The Exotic Rissole

TANVEER AHMED

NEWSOUTH

A NewSouth book

Published by
NewSouth Publishing
University of New South Wales Press Ltd
University of New South Wales
Sydney NSW 2052
AUSTRALIA
newsouthpublishing.com

© Tanveer Ahmed 2011
First published 2011

10 9 8 7 6 5 4 3 2 1

National Library of Australia
Cataloguing-in-Publication entry
  Author: Ahmed, Tanveer.
  Title: The exotic rissole/Tanveer Ahmed.
  ISBN: 978 1 74223 255 3 (pbk.)
  Subjects: Ahmed, Tanveer.
    Immigrants – Australia – Biography.
    Muslims – Australia – Biography.
  Dewey Number: 305.697

Design Josephine Pajor-Markus
Cover design Design by Committee
Cover images Bigstockphoto
Printer Ligare

This book is printed on paper using fibre supplied from plantation or sustainably managed forests.

Australian Government   Australia Council for the Arts

This project has been assisted by the Australian Government through the Australia Council for the Arts, its arts funding and advisory body.

For my parents,
Amma and Abba

Contents

Prologue

I loved everything about my best friend, Daryl. Ever since second grade, when my family had moved to Toongabbie, we sat next to each other in class and walked home together. I also called him Lynchy, having perfected the Australian practice of elongating someone's name with an 'o' or a 'y'. I admired his crew cut and was riveted by his rat's tail, which he sported with great confidence. I wished I could have one, but my parents were horrified at the idea, believing it would be my first step towards the juvenile justice system.

We had migrated from Bangladesh when I was five. My dad still cut my hair once a month, a ritual we undertook while I sat on a stool in the bathroom. Without fail he would remind me of how he cut his relatives' hair in the small Bangladeshi village he grew up in, a story that would coincide with another about him waking at dawn to sell rice at the local markets in order to fund his education. Once, when my mother came home and confessed to a fifty dollar haircut, he almost collapsed into his armchair. He was adamant, it seemed, that I would never pay for one.

Lynchy advised me that my father's foray into hairdressing had to stop. We were almost twelve years old and were beginning to take an interest in girls. My chances of meeting a girl were zip while my father was channelling 1970s rural Bangladeshi fashion through me.

Lynchy would visit my house every day after school and we'd ride our BMX bikes to the local creek. There we would play marbles, skim rocks across the water or play French cricket with a plastic bat. I had never visited his house. He always made excuses about his annoying older sister or said that his parents didn't like having guests. I didn't push it. I thought my parents were annoying, too, and I was embarrassed that my house always smelled like curry.

But Lynchy seemed to love hanging out at my house. He would sit with my adoring mother on a stool in our tiny kitchen and talk about school. He helped her make snacks and dip doughy mixtures into Indian spices. He said that all his family ate were rissoles, steak and baked potatoes. I looked at him with envy, wishing my mother would cook things like that.

Mum treated Daryl like her long-lost Aussie son, hand feeding him and stroking him across his blonde flat-top. 'You are a very nice boy, Dar-yl,' she would say. 'Not like my boy, who never eats his vegetable curry.'

I never felt jealous. I knew she was just being nice, because she often lamented how poorly Daryl did at school. She'd encourage us to do our homework together, but the chances of that happening were slim. I can't say I was ever disappointed. It was embarrassing to be good at school and

I tried to hide my academic abilities as much as possible. I even failed a couple of tests on purpose, but my teacher freaked out and thought about sending me to counselling. That was enough motivation for me to top the class again.

Once Lynchy had chowed down on his afternoon samosas, it was time for our daily ride to the creek. That was all our suburb really had. Back then, Toongabbie seemed to be home to the highest concentration of drug addicts, single mothers and ex-cons in all of Sydney, though I'm not sure there were Census figures to prove it. We learnt at school that the suburb's name means 'the place where waters meet', which just seemed like an Aboriginal euphemism for floods. The place is flat and low lying and it was often awash when the creek overflowed. Some people thought we lived there because the poverty and flooding resembled Bangladesh. The next year, when I started at a posh private school in the city, I was known as Tanny from Toony. Unsurprisingly, I'd take my tie and suit jacket off when I got off the train to walk home for fear of being abused.

It was on one of the very last days of primary school when Lynchy asked me to come over to his house. I was shocked. It felt like some kind of goodbye before we headed off to high school. For all our talk of staying friends, I thought his invitation was an admission that it would be futile.

'We'll still see each other, man,' I said, genuinely believing it. 'I'll still live in Toony.'

Lynchy reassured me my concerns had nothing to do with it. Asking me over was his mum's idea as a kind of repayment for all the food my mother had fed him. I nodded with approval. I longed to taste the mouth-watering promise of his mum's rissole, the delicate balance of mince, bread crumbs and egg. I'd asked at the local milk bar about the meaty concoction, but they said they didn't cook them anymore, and their fried potato scallops and Chiko rolls didn't excite me in the same way.

On the agreed day, Lynchy and I walked home from school to his white weatherboard house near the train station. There was a front patio where his long-haired, tattooed father used to sit and read car magazines, but he'd been gone for months. I'd often walked past and seen Lynchy's mother watering the garden, which consisted of a handful of struggling red azaleas planted in a zigzag.

She always smiled but she looked like she had bigger worries in her life. Lynchy's older sister, Stacey, never paid much attention to me, once telling me that I was too short for any girls to like me. Her comment helped cement me as a loyal sidekick to Lynchy's lead role in the Stacey Slagging Society. 'Stacey's face is a zit factory,' we'd cackle before scurrying away on our bikes, or 'Stacey is meeting her boyfriend at the parole office.'

That afternoon, only Lynchy's mum was home. Stacey was still at work. She was a hairdresser. Daryl had told me recently that his dad no longer lived with them and I was confused and asked dumb questions about why. He told me about his parents' separation while we sat by the creek and gave each other horse bites, slapping each other on the leg. It was a rare, tender moment between two boys, except for the fact I had no idea what divorce was. He said his parents fought a lot and his mum thought it was better they lived apart.

I didn't get it. As far as I could see, my parents had barely anything you could call a relationship. They would visit family friends and occasionally watch Indian movies together, but I could see there was little else they had in common. But most of the other Bangladeshi couples I knew weren't much different, so I was never worried or confused about their apparent mismatch. My father would just work in the garden and tell me to go and study while my mother did the housework, presiding over complex dishes in the kitchen and making me and my little sister eat all the time. My parents fought a lot, too, yet they seemed to have no problems staying together.

Lynchy and I sat at the breakfast table while his mum unloaded the dishwasher, chatting to us about our day. I watched in awe. My father thought dishwashers were an expensive luxury good and bred laziness. Lynchy's mum had told me to call her Bridget. She had weathered, lined skin like many older Australians who had spent too much time in the sun. Her heavy-lidded eyes and furrowed forehead gave her a melancholy edge. I thought she looked kind of sad. She patted me on the head, just like my mother did with Lynchy. I liked it. She told me I must have been really smart to win a scholarship and wished me well at my new school. My parents never told me I was smart. I was thrilled.

I had been to very few houses where white Australians lived. All my other friends were migrants from other countries and we often defined ourselves in terms of our difference to 'Aussies'. There was Larsen, the Filipino kid who loved basketball and couldn't say 'f'. 'Puck you,' he would say when he was angry. His family loved karaoke and I could hear them singing on the weekends when I knocked on the door. I once ate tripe at their house without knowing.

There was a guy from Thailand who we knew as Jimmy Thai because nobody could say his surname, Chungsiriwat. His parents ran a place called Thai-Pan. They were pioneers in the art of puns in Thai restaurant names. Jimmy could kickbox and was famous for breaking wind on demand. Other kids would travel from all over the suburb to see him perform his biological feats of flatulence. Once he had a crowd of almost twenty kids, holding skateboards and leaning on their BMX bikes, to see him perform his famous machine-gun fart. He even signed autographs.

My Turkish mate, Fazil, would help his dad manage their mobile doner kebab business which they ran out of the back of a caravan. I used to love eating the leftover meat, which they kept in the freezer. His mum reheated it, wrapped the strips of lamb in Lebanese bread and we'd munch on it while we played video games. I later learnt his father was on workers' compensation for a neck injury, as was an uncle. I felt sorry for these people who seemed to disproportionately suffer injuries in car accidents.

Sitting there with Lynchy waiting for our afternoon tea, I looked at Bridget's short cropped hair with interest.

My mother always kept her hair long. Aussies are definitely different, I thought to myself. Lynchy's house smelled a bit like their dog, a big German shepherd that intermittently sniffed my shoes. They also had an air conditioner and a SodaStream machine. I was amazed. My parents would never buy such wondrous things. Bridget sensed my awe. 'Would you like a fizzy orange drink, Tanny?' she asked. I nodded mutely and she dropped two ice cubes into a glass. Within minutes I was tasting a piece of heaven.

'I know your mother loves gardening,' Bridget said, making conversation. 'I can't keep my azaleas alive in the heat. I should get her to help.' Daryl sat beside me quietly, looking as embarrassed as I felt when he was friendly with my mother, but I was riveted by the foreign surroundings. Then Lynchy pushed his fingers through his hair and boasted about having been checked for head lice at school and coming out clean. Bridget patted him on the head before asking me more questions.

'Have you been back to Bangladesh, Tanny?' she said. Daryl had told her where we'd come from, after lengthy lessons at my place where I showed him where the country was on the map and how it was formed after repeated war between India and Pakistan.

'Mum, did you know Bangladesh became independent in 1971, a few years before I was born? Heaps of people died and stuff,' Darryl said, jumping in first.

'I've been there but I got bad diarrhoea,' I said, hoping to impress. 'I preferred the villages to the crowded, dirty cities. More peaceful.'

Bridget laughed heartily. 'You just made me wish I'd travelled more, Tanny. Daryl's father never had any interest in the world beyond, only his tools.'

Lynchy bowed his head and a frown appeared. I felt embarrassed and sad for him as the mood in the room turned sour for an instant. Bridget patted him on the head again and motioned to some food on a plate. 'I put some rissoles in sandwiches for you two. Dig in.'

Lynchy grabbed two and handed me one. We bit into them while sipping our SodaStream-manufactured soft drink. A rush came over me as I tasted the exotic, spice-free rissole bursting across my taste buds. It was worth the wait.

In spite of my youthful, optimistic hopes of lasting friendship, Daryl and I grew apart over the following year. I was pulled into a new world of studying Latin and singing hymns at the private school I'd won a place at. We met up a couple of times but we didn't seem to have much in common anymore. He didn't have a great deal to say. Looking back now, I guess he was coming to terms with the fact that he barely saw his dad. By the end of the year, Bridget decided to sell their house and move to the north coast. I never saw him again.

I often thought of Daryl in my first year of high school, imagining him riding his bike along the beachfront of his new hometown in his black Led Zeppelin T-shirt. I still think of him, grateful for my first, significant connection in a foreign land. He was someone who helped bridge my sense of difference.

After some gentle urging on my part, my mother taught

herself how to cook rissoles, although she mixed chilli and turmeric paste into them. Now, I think my life's been a bit like that mashed up Aussie tucker – a heady mix of cultures, professions and experiences. I cook rissoles for my own children sometimes, adding just a hint of spice and my own contribution to the mix, a healthy dollop of melted cheese.

The only issue is that my wife calls them fritters.

1
Arrival Allergy

I remember sitting on my sari-clad mother's lap watching the doctor draw up an injection. He had turned to his side to block my view of the syringe, but I could still see it from the corner of my eye. The silver needle shimmered in the dim light of the surgery. I watched as the doctor forced out a short spray of liquid, the same liquid he was about to thrust into my body.

Dr Sharma was a middle-aged Indian man with wisps of grey hair. My mother had brought me to his Harris Park surgery for some compulsory vaccinations. He wore a white lab coat and a black stethoscope hung around his neck. He had a pot belly which he tried to conceal by buttoning up the middle section of his coat. He tried to interest me in playing with the stethoscope. I was focussed on the needle.

Dr Sharma spoke to my mother in what I thought was Bengali, but which turned out to be Hindi. She had once told me it was the language of Indian movies which I knew consisted of lots of dancing and singing, something I couldn't picture Dr Sharma doing.

'We are from, er, Bangladesh, you know?' she said. Her spoken English lacked confidence and she couldn't stop herself from throwing in Bengali words like 'acha' and 'haa', which mean OK and yes. This was despite the fact that she worked as an English teacher back in Bangladesh, even teaching me for a short period while I was in kindergarten. I wondered why the English in this country sounded so different to hers. It didn't sound anything like the BBC, which my father would listen to on the radio sometimes.

It had been barely a week since I'd arrived in Sydney with my parents. My father had accepted a job offer in Australia. None of our relatives had heard of the place. If anyone left Bangladesh they moved to the UK.

'Ki korba Australia the? Why do you want to live with kangaroos?' asked my maternal uncle, Lattu, days before we were planning to leave.

Now that we had arrived, we were boarding with some family friends, Rama and Mrinal. My parents knew them from their university days and had helped arrange their marriage back in Bangladesh. Mrinal had also taught my mother as a student at boarding school. As a result my mother called him Sir, and I called him Sir Mama, which means Uncle Sir. Mrinal and Rama had bought their first car weeks earlier in preparation for our arrival.

They had migrated two years earlier and lived at Harris Park, a long way from the city where my father had begun work. I was very conscious of my dark skin. Here everyone looked taller and whiter. I missed the constant throng of relatives and affection that was the norm in Bangladesh. There were lots of red brick flats and very few people compared with home. The roads were wide and clean and dominated by the sound of cars whooshing past. I was surprised to see no rickshaws.

'Australia is too rich to have rickshaws, Shuvo,' my mother said. Shuvo was one of my nicknames. I called her Amma, which is mother in Bengali.

We had already been visited by several Bangladeshi families, people I'd never met before. There was the jolly Shahadud Bhai, Hasmat Ali the champion bridge player and the softly spoken Jainal, an ex flatmate of my father. My parents would refer to them all as Bhai, which means brother. They all pressed upon us plastic containers full of food, as if we needed urgent nourishment, and talked sadly about how difficult it was to find mustard oil and good cooking spices. The women encouraged my mother, Latifa, to watch the television show *Sons and Daughters*. They seemed unusually happy to see us, laughing and smiling with gusto.

I watched Dr Sharma warily. I was five years old and only knew I was about to get an injection for the second time in a week. I had walked off the plane full of excitement, carrying a remote control car bought on stopover in Singapore and wearing my Six Million Dollar Man jacket. It was my favourite show as a child in Bangladesh. But now the thrill was dimming and I blamed Australia for the needles, for my lack of English skills, for the loss of my friends and for having had an apple confiscated at the airport.

Dr Sharma pointed to a photograph on the wall next to his framed medical degree. It was a portrait of a boy with a bowl haircut, who looked slightly older than me, a girl with pigtails and their mother, who looked uncannily like Dr Sharma's secretary. He told me in Bengali that they'd arrived in Australia soon after his son's birth in India.

'You will love Australia and forget Bangladesh soon, little boy,' he said, patting me on the head.

I nodded.

'Yes, he will be loving this country when he is older, I think,' Amma said, not sounding very confident.

Clearly this enjoyment lay some way into the future because soon after Dr Sharma's tender interlude he leapt towards me, telling my mother to hold me still. In a swift and efficient movement he lifted my short sleeved shirt and slid the needle into my arm.

I winced in pain, erupted into tears and plunged my head into my mother's bosom. Needles were sizeable and painful in 1980. My shoulder throbbed in agony. Doctor Sharma chuckled as he patted me on the head again. When I finally looked up, he was holding a red, bean-shaped sweet in his outstretched hand. I took it without hesitation and swallowed it quickly, offered him a tentative smile before returning to the solace of my mother's chest.

As we walked out of the surgery, I felt a sudden gush of warmth come across my body. At first I thought I had wet myself. It began in my stomach before spreading right through my middle, like a bomb exploding internally but in slow motion. The injections I'd had before hadn't felt anything like this. Maybe the odd-shaped sweet was to blame. Now I regretted grabbing it so impulsively.

'Amma, I'm getting hot and want to vomit,' I said in

Bengali, holding my stomach.

'Going to the doctor is hard at first, but good later,' she replied, bending down to pick me up in her arms. She tried to distract me by pointing to shops across the road with Arabic writing on the windows, familiar to me as the language of the Koran.

By now there was a gigantic itch beginning to overwhelm my entire body. I could feel my face puffing up, as if someone was blowing it up like a balloon. Soon I had trouble breathing and gasped for air. Amma looked down at me in her arms. Her face turned red before she let out a yelp of panic and ran back toward the surgery. I knew then that something was wrong.

Mrs Sharma was making a cup of tea. She took one look at me and immediately rushed into the doctor's rooms, knocking her cup of tea onto the carpet. There was a mirror on the wall and I could see raised splotches of red on my face and neck.

My mother was breathing as hard as I was and repeatedly saying 'Ore-bap', which translates as a worried kind of 'wow'. She was known within her family as a worrywart but it was justified this time. 'I wish your abba was here right now,' she said, referring to my father, who had begun his first week of work.

My heart was racing and I was desperate to itch myself. I wished the Six Million Dollar Man would save me.

Dr Sharma flung open the door and motioned for us to come back into his rooms. He remained calm and counselled my mother. I didn't really understand, but my mother told me that Dr Sharma thought I was having a reaction to the vaccine. He felt my wrist, took my blood pressure and put the stethoscope on my back to listen to my breathing. He told me in Bengali that I would be fine, before emitting another chuckle. I started to relax, as did my mother who began to breathe normally.

Dr Sharma swiftly drew up another injection and plunged it straight into my arm. Australia was feeling like the land of injections to me. I barely noticed the pain this time, distracted by my itch. There was no jellybean.

Like magic, within seconds my breathing began to improve and the itch settled. Amma pointed out some small blisters on my body.

'No more red spots tomorrow, little boy,' the doctor said, shaking his head and pointing at the lesions. Then he gave me a big smile and a hearty hug. My life had been saved, it seemed. The chubby Indian man in a lab coat was my new hero. But despite the explanation offered by my doctor, my suspicion of jellybeans remained. I avoided them for several years.

'I think you might be allergic ... Er, your body doesn't like this injection.' Then he looked at my mother. 'Remember the name, tikhe?' he said, saying all right in Bengali. 'It's called tetanus.'

The word hit me like a sledgehammer. In spite of my limited English, it was a word I recognised. Tetanus. Or te-ti-nas, which is how Bangladeshis pronounce it. Only a few months before I had heard it screamed in anguish.

Back in Bangladesh, my best friend Rojon and I would

chase chickens as they scavenged and squawked around the shared courtyard of our housing estate, which had four brick buildings with tin roofs, each with one bedroom and a living room. We'd bathe in a closet-sized bathroom. Amma would pour water over me from a pot, heating it up on the stove during the winter. There was also a toilet there, a sculpted hole in the floor which I would squat over.

A rusty well supplied water for all the families. There was a large mango tree in the middle of the courtyard that provided precious shade, a saviour when the scorching heat of summer made it hard to even go outside. The estate lay on a street known as Kazi Avenue, on the edge of Dhaka's old city with its narrow lanes, old Mughal ruins and the constant sound of rickshaws and their ringing bells. There was a butcher next door where the carcasses of cows and goats hung off hooks in the open air.

I was born in a nearby hospital. Instead of lying in a cot, I was nursed by my grandmother all night for fear of being kidnapped, a common occurrence in the hospital. I was at greater risk because I was both male and relatively fair-skinned, both prized traits. My birth came within days of the assassination of the country's president and his entire family. They were murdered in their sleep. Sheikh Mujib was known as the father of the nation. His death was part of a bloody military coup, as the country was teetering on the edge of famine and bankruptcy. Betrayal and revenge was in the air. While I was suckling at my mother's breast, the country was on the verge of civil war.

There were always people from my father's village staying with us while they passed through the capital. While they were usually close relatives, the term could stretch a long way. There was Mozhar, who I called 'Boro Kaka', which means 'Big Uncle'; he was my father's eldest brother. He spent weeks at a time there. There was also Mintu Bhai, who was just some guy from the same district, and even Waheed, the local bus driver, came to stay. Our house was like a one-room motel.

This tension between immediate and extended family began well before my birth, soon after my parents were married in a modest function in my mother's university dormitory. Their first home together was a tiny room that was partitioned with my father's brother, Boro Kaka, sleeping on the other side. A week into his marriage, my father bought a small fan and angled it carefully in the middle of the room, balanced on his textbooks, so that it would cool both his brother and his own new wife simultaneously, a distribution of affection that would remain controversial well into the future.

Rojon had big round cheeks and always wore a white skullcap on his head. He usually wore a panjabi, a cream, embroidered cotton robe that fell down to the knees, the traditional garment for Bangladeshi males. The youngest of three boys, Rojon was only a year or so older than me. He used to hold me upside down in the courtyard and the servant girls would laugh at me.

Many of the servants weren't much older than me. They wore the same raggy clothes each day and didn't attend school. They cooked and cleaned and returned to their villages during the holidays. Everybody I knew had servants. They were virtually part of the family. 'Some families have too many children and can't look after them all,' my mother had told me once, pointing to our servant girl Lulu. 'They are very poor but you must treat them like your own family.'

Rojon wasn't a bully; he was like an older brother, reminding me who was the more senior from time to time. He once ran out onto the road to pull me away from an oncoming cow cart. I was still gouged by a horn. Amma still points to the scar on my forehead to remind me what a hyperactive child I was. I was known for my big brown eyes and she was grateful that the horns hadn't lodged into one of them instead.

Rojon's father, Nabil, worked on the banks of the nearby river, an offshoot of the famous Ganges. He was a ship breaker, pulling apart the metal sections of old ships and selling them for scrap. While my father came home in a suit carrying a briefcase full of files and documents, Rojon's dad returned from work with cuts and grazes from the rusty hulls of the decaying boats. I imagined him to be a captain steering ships through the river and seas, a job that seemed far more exciting than my father's.

Our mothers ventured out to the nearby markets together and would return with bags of rice, green vegetables I didn't like the taste of, like zucchini and broccoli, and, on special occasions, whole chickens or goats, which would be slaughtered by either of the fathers. Once I saw a chicken running around the courtyard with blood pouring from where its head had been. I wasn't meant to see things like that; I'd happened to look out the window of Rojon's house after I was put there by a servant.

Rojon's mother, Khadija, was very religious and usually wore a full length black burqa. She carried beads which she would fiddle with while praying. She'd given me a set but I lost them down a nearby drain. She kept telling me that Allah was watching and that when I got older and attended the local high school I would learn to pray and recite the Koran. Once, when Rojon and I were playing hide and seek, I had fallen asleep behind our sofa. I was lost, nowhere to be found, and there was a frantic search to find me. Finally I was found by Aunty Khadija, who woke me up. I remember opening my eyes, looking up at the figure of an imposing black-robed woman and screaming in terror. She was like an Islamic Grim Reaper. My mother never wore such clothing, nor did most of my other female relatives.

The day that remains the dominant memory of my childhood in Bangladesh was hot and dry. Uncle Lattu, my mother's brother, was staying with us. He'd bought a map of the world and had stuck it to the wall to show me where my parents were taking me. My father had applied for migration to a range of places and was deciding between Australia and Iraq. My mother was trying to convince my father that Australia would be better for my future.

Uncle Lattu pointed to a large island at the bottom of the map. I had never heard of Australia. I only knew of America, India and London, places I'd heard people bragging about visiting. They often did something called a PhD there, which I knew was very impressive. While Iraq was closer, it was harder to find on the map than the more visible Australia. But if we decided on Iraq perhaps visits back home would be easier.

Apparently my father's qualifications as an actuary were very rare and he was in great demand throughout the world. I couldn't see why this was a good thing. To cheer me up, Uncle Lattu took me and Rojon to a park where we played with homemade slingshots. A thick rubber band was tied to a twig and we flicked small stones at trees and small birds. Rojon was very skilled with a slingshot and managed to hit some sparrows. 'Congratulations, Rojon. Khubi bhalo,' said Uncle Lattu. 'You will one day compete in the Olympics.' We carried the mangled birds back home.

When we returned late that morning, our fathers were both at work and the heat inspired laziness among the rest of us. Amma sat on a stool cutting tomatoes on a boti, a crescent shaped knife which jutted upwards from a wooden block. Next door, Rojon told his mother he had a headache and that his leg felt strange. She had just finished praying on a mat inside. 'Kub groom,' his mother said, telling him to come inside. 'Bhithore asho.'

Hours passed. I walked in, wanting to play. Rojon hadn't held me upside down all day. He looked pale and withdrawn. His mother felt his forehead. Now he had a fever and looked stiff and straight, so she took him to a nearby doctor. My mother felt my forehead, too, worried that I might have caught something similar.

When they returned an hour later, Rojon still looked stiff and tired. 'The doctor sahib said it is a virus and should pass, inshallah,' said his mother, rolling the beads in her hand faster than ever. He was put to bed inside their house.

That night, my mother cooked our conquered sparrows in spices with some potatoes. Uncle Lattu and I munched on their small bones. My father returned late from work and it wasn't long before he and my mother began their customary argument about managing money and whether we could afford to fly overseas.

'Babur Abba,' my mother would address him, which means father of a baby boy. 'You buy nothing for me and your son and spend it all on your relatives.'

'Oh, yes, I do nothing all day and somebody else pays for this house and food,' my father would retort.

Fleeing the scene, I went next door with Uncle Lattu to offer some of the food to Rojon and his family. They were all crowded around the bed where Rojon lay, debating whether to take him to hospital. Rojon's parents worried that going to a hospital might do more harm than good, reciting old horror stories of hospital errors that had killed or maimed people they knew. His mother started twirling her beads and praying to God, reciting Arabic phrases over and over.

'Auzu billah. Bismillah,' she said, repeating the Arabic prayer anxiously, holding her cupped hands together over their prized velvet hardback copy of the Koran. It was usually kept locked away in a drawer.

Rojon looked even stiffer than before. He was complaining of spasms in his leg. 'Kub batha,' he said, pointing to his teeth and gums and grimacing in pain.

He gave me a small smile when I told him how tasty the sparrow was. When my father was called, they decided there was no choice but to take him to hospital and they disappeared quickly into the night on a rickshaw, its ringing bell fading as it accelerated away. I remember Rojon was resting his head on his father's shoulder, his white skullcap a pale shape in the dark.

I woke the next morning to find my mother frowning over a plate of rice. She hugged me more firmly than usual, then sat me down at our lone table and looked into my eyes. 'Your father came back from the hospital very late when you were sleeping. Rojon is very sick,' she said in Bengali, before adding that his back had begun to arch wildly, his jaw was clamped tight and the muscles that controlled his breathing were shutting down. 'He must have stepped on a nail or a piece of metal a few days ago,' she explained.

I couldn't remember anything. That kind of thing was a daily event for us. Later that morning a large number of people arrived at our shared compound. Many of them were unfamiliar, but I could make out Rojon's older brothers among them. People were trying to reassure them, patting them on their shoulders.

Suddenly there was a loud wailing and screaming from Rojon's mother, who was being held by several men. 'Oh, Allah! Allah, what have you done?' she shouted desperately to the sky, waving her hands violently.

I was desperate to see what had happened. I followed Amma to our front door and then tried to run out, but she pulled me back. She tried to block my view but I caught a glimpse of Rojon's father carrying a body inside their house. My father was holding the legs. In an instant I recognised Rojon's clothes, his white skullcap.

I didn't understand what was happening but started crying anyway. I could hear more screaming through the shared walls. Amma went next door, and returned in tears. Then she started packing some bags. 'We must go to your uncle's house for a few days, Shuvo. Abba will stay here,' she said, dressing me quickly in pants and a jacket.

As I was rushed out, the crowd assembling in the court-yard was growing bigger and people were beginning to pray. Two days later, when we came home, I learnt I would never see Rojon again. He had died of something called tetanus and had been buried in his father's village in a far away district. The word was etched into my memory. Te-ti-nas. I knew to stay away from whatever it was.

'Maybe we shouldn't have played in the dirt, Amma?' I asked my mother.

'Baba, there was nothing you did wrong,' she said, patting me on the head before taking me in her arms. 'God works in strange ways.'

Although I had seen chickens slaughtered and the sparrows shot down with a stone, I had little understanding of the meaning of death. For weeks I expected Rojon to return, thinking he had just gone into the village. In the meantime, my mother convinced my father that Australia would offer me better opportunities, despite his view that an Islamic country like Iraq was preferable. In the few months before we left Bangladesh, I started wetting the bed.

Now, I'm not sure if my memories are real or imagined – perhaps they are just fragments of stories that my mother has told me. But given my response to Dr Sharma's vaccine, it seems my body may have remembered the events more clearly.

2
My Favourite Teacher

Amma always wore a sari. Her favourite was an orange floral one, made of a special silk called jamdani. Soon after we arrived in Australia, her close friend, Rama, bought her a muu-muu style dress which was also covered in flowers. My mother wore it gleefully through the streets, taking great pride in her single piece of Western clothing. She'd pick up the groceries for the week in the pink frilly dress, blissfully unaware of the bemused looks that her outfit inspired.

When my father returned home from work, she told him, 'Desh kub shundoor,' meaning the country was beautiful. 'The people here are friendly and laugh happily when they meet me,' she explained. It wasn't until she met Rama at the local train station one afternoon and witnessed the look of shock on her friend's face that she was made aware of the niche purpose of her clothing.

'Minu, that dress is a nightie,' Rama said, giggling, calling my mother by her nickname. She walked her back home so that Amma could change.

My father's first job in Sydney was for a life insurance

company called Tyndall. They'd written to him in Bangladesh after an actuary friend of his from Switzerland had referred him to potential occupational suitors in Australia. On his first day, he wore a grey polyester suit and thick, black-rimmed glasses with photochromatic lenses which transformed into sunglasses when exposed to daylight. For Abba, it was like wearing a little piece of modernity in an outfit otherwise arranged for thrift.

In July 1980, very soon after Abba started in his new job, we moved into our own two-bedroom flat. We were still in Harris Park, on Brisbane Street. Furnished courtesy of the Smith Family, we had a velvety orange couch, a worn but functional double mattress on a springy, wooden base which I shared with my parents and a small metal lamp with a round plastic cover. We also received rusty pots and pans which my mother cradled with joy. This most modest of abodes was transformed into our very own palace.

Each morning Amma woke early to prepare food for my father. She made paratha bread, which is dough fried in ghee oil, with dahl and curried chicken.

'Babur Abba!' she'd shout out to my dad. It means father of Babu, which was the nickname I was given as a baby. It literally means baby. It seems like an obscure tradition, but it was no longer proper to call my father by his name after I was born. His role and identity had shifted.

Then Amma would prepare me a breakfast fit for a child emperor, spacing out three separate plates: one with an omelette, another with a vermicelli-based sweet called suji and the last with flat bread. She would roll the bread with a filling of either egg or suji before gently feeding me by hand.

I started kindergarten soon after we arrived. I was petrified. Amma carried me in her arms to the local school, Rosehill Public. I had just turned six. The teachers were horrified that I was so mollycoddled. They wondered if my development had been delayed. After some questioning about my abilities, my mother disintegrated into panic. The Australian accent was an enormous challenge for her.

'They talk so fast and don't even open their mouths,' she'd say in Bengali.

My teachers spoke gently to her and asked if I was slow. She shook her head profusely. 'No, my boy is not stupid. He is just new to this country.'

I was immediately placed into a special class for newly arrived immigrants who couldn't speak English. Mrs Henderson was our teacher. She was a tall brunette with thickset glasses that she often lowered to the tip of her nose, peering with fascination at her students as they attempted to name objects on the flash cards.

'This one ... it is chicken,' I said, while Mrs Henderson pointed to a cow.

'That be a house,' I said confidently while gazing at a picture of a saddled horse.

Every day Mrs Henderson would patiently recite the alphabet to the class, which was made up of me and seven others. Hour after hour she held up pictures and valiantly deciphered a host of confused phrases in different languages. There was Ramazan, an overweight Lebanese boy whose parents ran a kebab store. We became close friends despite his attempt to sit on me and crush me in the playground on my first day. Tinh was a Vietnamese girl, a few years older than me, who wore a red cardigan and matching ribbons in her hair every day. There were several others of varying ages from countries I had never heard of like Malta and Yugoslavia. It was like a mini United Nations where we fought for linguistic recognition. To Mrs Henderson's credit, none of us stayed in the class for more than a few weeks.

The only English I knew was 'I want water'. I had few friends initially, but managed to remain well hydrated. I was also a regular visitor to the schoolyard toilet.

Mrs Henderson helped me expand on my water line to include the concept of a glass, the notion of drinking as opposed to swallowing or sipping, being thirsty and even the meaning of spillage, a term I was able to illustrate with ease. By the end of the first week, my one line had become a soliloquy.

'I want a cold glass of unspilled water to help my thirsty, dry mouth,' I announced proudly to the class one day.

Mrs Henderson had a soothing voice which calmed our nerves as we slowly recited the alphabet. I had never felt so stupid in my life, but she had a way of making it all feel normal. She would meet with my mother at the end of each week and advise her on ways I could be helped at home.

'You can give him homework to improve his English, Mrs Ahmed,' Mrs Henderson said. 'He learns new words every day.'

Amma was pleased that the teachers no longer suspected I was slow. She started reading to me from newspapers, sticking labels on knives, chairs and the bathtub and actively made me watch television to hear the Australian accent. Her favourite show was *Prisoner* and together we'd watch the big, round women in jail ironing their clothes and showing off their tattoos. I later had an overweight, red-headed babysitter called Doreen and I was sure was one of the cast. 'Hurry up, slow coach!' she used to yell while walking me to school, determined to make me less of a mummy's boy.

I left Mrs Henderson's class after almost a month. My English was still below par for kindergarten and I stumbled through the rest of the year, helped by my friend Ramazan in navigating the social complexities of the school playground. He introduced me to salt and vinegar chips and to chasing girls. He offered inducements of his parents' felafel and shaved kebab meat but the offer was rarely taken up by other pupils, although I had no such reluctance. I brought him my mother's paratha bread, which we ate together in the playground.

I remained shy, often hiding behind Ramazan to avoid speaking to the other kids, but my confidence grew as I slowly learned to form full sentences. While my classroom results were only mediocre, I was allowed to progress to first grade with the rest of my class. I would run into Mrs Henderson when she supervised the playground during recess or lunch. She once brought me an apple and asked me to name three other bits of fruit.

My mother remained very worried about my progress and met with the principal every month for an update. She obsessively checked my homework and conducted dictation tests from newspaper clippings. My father took me to Flemington markets every Saturday morning where he tested my mathematical knowledge when buying fish and vegetables.

'If I buy two kilos of mullet and each kilo is four dollars – very expensive today – how much does it cost?' he said.

'Abba, the smell is horrible,' I replied, before eventually answering.

After a few months of early morning treks watching my father hunt for food bargains, I stayed in the car to avoid his maths challenges, and to keep clear of the fishy pong.

At the end of first grade, the principal announced to my mother that I'd come first in the class. My mother didn't believe her, thinking it was an attempt to make her feel better, that it was code for me having only improved satisfactorily. When she relayed the news to her friend, Rama, her suspicions were supported.

'Does she mean first from the top, or first from the bottom?' Rama asked her. My mother knew she wasn't joking.

But when Amma came to pick me up one day, Mrs Henderson explained that I really had done well, giving my dumbstruck mother a card of congratulations. It had a picture of a glass of water on the front.

3
Bald and Dangerous

I don't remember being jealous, but a baby photograph of my sister suggests her arrival had an impact. I had poked her eyes out with a pen, leaving gaping holes. I don't remember doing it. As time went on I moved on to the real thing and stuck chewing gum in her hair, farted in her face while she lay on the couch and threw tennis balls at her head in the backyard. I also tortured her Cabbage Patch doll with skewers and a lighter.

Tania was born late at night in Westmead hospital in March, 1981. She arrived with thin, reddish hair, fair skin and hazel eyes. She reminded me of cousins on my father's side, children with brown hair and light complexions who ran around the village waving sticks and chasing farm animals. The story was that they were a throwback to the Persian conquerors of India, the Moghul empire that produced the Taj Mahal.

My mother was nine weeks' pregnant when we flew to Australia. My sister's name was chosen for its transferability between cultures. In Arabic it meant fairy queen. As a baby, Tania was often dressed in a pink top with 'Just Peachy' on it.

Six months after Tania was born, Amma started working in the filing section of the Taxation Office. She had to commute by train to the city and wore trousers and a shirt borrowed from her friend Rama. For several weeks she roamed the offices, too frightened to speak for fear of embarrassing herself, before befriending a Filipino woman called Andrea. She and Andrea were the only non-white people in the office. Within a month of starting, they were both transferred to the Pyrmont office.

Walking frantically to find their new building, armed only with the knowledge that it was near the pub, the two slight women of Asian origin resorted to desperately asking people in the street for directions.

'Could you please tell to me where the pub is?' my mother asked repeatedly. 'We have to find the pub, please. It is very important.' It was nine o'clock in the morning, and the two Taxation Office employees were met with looks of shock by morning commuters worried about the welfare of the young, ethnic, female alcoholics.

Amma was miserable at work and guilty about leaving her new baby daughter in the care of others. She dreamt of the care she would have received from the extended family if we'd remained in Bangladesh. But we needed the money desperately. For six months we did without a fridge because my father needed to pay for the dowry and wedding of his only sister in Bangladesh.

Tania didn't forget the many hours she spent at daycare either and often reminded my mother about her memories of feeling abandoned. While I was jealous of her looks and remain convinced that her Australian nutrition helped make her much taller, I'd received my mother's undivided attention as a child.

Two years after we had arrived in Australia, we moved from Harris Park to Toongabbie. Our new house was bought for $50,000 from another Bangladeshi family, a price my father had bargained fiercely for. Amma always said his tough, deprived upbringing meant he would fight for every cent in a negotiation. I once saw him get shoved to the ground by an angry shop assistant in a discount luggage store in the city while he negotiated for a suitcase. The assistant perceived him as rude, but my dad was just talking the talk as he would have done in Bangladesh.

Soon after she started kindergarten, my father shaved Tania's head – against her will, unsurprisingly. She screamed through the whole procedure, her face drenched with tears. My parents and family friends were concerned that her light coloured hair was too flimsy, not as healthy as the usual Bangladeshi black. Her first days at school were distraught ones as she faced the scrutiny of the other five-year-olds with a bald head.

Tania was Toongabbie Public School's own Sinead O'Connor, without the singing ability. I was in sixth class and visited my traumatised sister at lunchtime in between handball games with Lynchy. The other children kept asking her where her hair was while most teachers avoided the subject for fear she had cancer and was receiving treatment. She started wearing a cap but her teacher made her take if off during class.

Tania's hair grew back within a few weeks. My parents were convinced that the new sprouts were both darker and thicker and congratulated themselves on their good judgement, despite the obvious trauma inflicted upon Tania. Family friends like Rama also agreed Tania's hair was darker and healthier. It looked no different to me.

It was then that I got an inkling that Old World tradition and social conservatism was going to be a part of our lives, and that my sister was likely to be the one more harshly affected. There were bound to be other occasions when what my parents saw as protection of the fairer sex amounted to suppression.

The gap of six years between us was too great for us to be close friends, and not enough for me to become anything resembling a father figure. I did feel protective, though, and for the one year we attended the same school we walked home together. It was 1986, the centenary of the school's founding. To celebrate, we dressed in nineteenth century English-style outfits. We received costume instructions from our teachers and my mother cut up a pair of my grey trousers, transforming them into knickerbockers, which were complemented by long socks and braces. My sister wore a chequered dress with a frilly, round bonnet, like Little Miss Muffet. There we were, two Bangladeshi children dressed for Victorian England in the western suburbs of Sydney.

When we first returned to Bangladesh, Tania was almost five and I was eleven. She had trouble communicating while I had remained fluent in Bengali. We were both a little overwhelmed by the poverty, traffic and lack of Western comforts. None of our relatives had showers and bathing was still carried out with the help of a bucket of water. We dreamt of eating McDonald's and sang jingles to each other to sustain ourselves. While riding a rickshaw in Dhaka, I spotted golden arches in the distance.

'There, there, there! McDonald's!' Tania and I begged in stereo, only to arrive to see that both the logo and name had been ripped off. It was McDonald's, the Chinese restaurant.

On the same trip, my maternal grandmother presented Tania with a white baby goat. We called my grandmother Nani, a bit like Nonna for Italians. She was a lot like my mother – forever worried, dramatic and affectionate all at the same time. When we visited she continually inquired about our bodily functions, anxious about any imminent bouts of diarrhoea. She would often be waiting outside the bathroom with a glass of salty water in her hand.

'Pathla paikana?' she'd say with a gentle tilt of her head, a look of great concern in her eyes, asking if my poo was runny. Each visit to the toilet was a keenly scrutinised performance.

Nani always dressed in a plain white sari and tended to my ailing grandfather, who usually sat in a wooden chair outside his room accompanied by plates of food. She married him when she was twelve years old, soon after the end of World War Two and within a few months of Indian partition. At the stroke of twelve one night in 1947, India separated from East Bengal, which would eventually become a province of Pakistan. Because their village, Dihi, was located right on the eastern Indian border, my grandparents remember hundreds of thousands of people frantically crossing when the new territories were formed. Many were murdered and killed by their fellow countrymen burning with religious zeal, Hindu or Muslim. Now, border police wearing green uniforms and holding menacing rifles could be seen a few kilometres away in the distance. Their job was to try and stop the many illegal travellers and smugglers crossing in both directions. Despite the presence of the guards, Dihi was a pleasant place, leafy and green, the village surrounded by pine trees and a narrow river. This was where my mother grew up.

When Nani gave Tania the gift of a baby goat, she was euphoric and held it in her arms all day. 'I want to take it home and show my class,' she told me, brimming with excitement. She fed it leaves from the large mango tree next to the mud brick kitchen and bathed it under the tube well, the village tap that sucked water from deep underground.

'Shiggiri abar asho,' Nani told Tania, promising to take good care of the little horned creature, and urging her to return soon.

When we arrived back in Australia, my parents felt Tania's affection for the goat was a sign our household needed more pets. Proceeding with caution, we welcomed a goldfish as the first non-human member of our family. Within months it met a tragic end – we had forgotten to feed it and found it floating peacefully in our glass vase-cum-makeshift aquarium.

We attempted to sooth the heartbreak with a pet budgerigar that sang joyfully in our family room for almost a year before it also met an untimely end via the concurrence of a cage with its door left ajar and a hungry neighbour's cat. The tabby paraded out of the house with green feathers clearly visible around its mouth as if it were an extra in a Sylvester and Tweety cartoon. Tania cried for hours, demanded one minute's silence at dinner and a proper burial. The silence lasted twenty seconds before I exploded into fits of laughter and was punished with no television or video games for the following week.

When we returned to Bangladesh several years later, Tania was swelling with excitement in anticipation of seeing her beloved baby grown into a fully formed adult goat. She carried a photo of her cradling it on the village porch. From what I could tell, my parents didn't see the disaster coming at all. There was no question the goat would serve its utilitarian purpose in the end. But nobody thought of explaining this inevitable outcome to my sister.

When we arrived in Dihi late in the afternoon we were informed there was a great feast planned in Tania's honour. As part of the festivities marking our visit, the goat had been sacrificed that morning, its throat slit on the banks of the nearby pond. The task of explaining the calamity fell to my mother, who broke the news to Tania in a quiet room alongside my Nani, pleading desperately for Tania's forgiveness.

The idea of Tania seeing the animal as a long-distance pet and looking forward to a reunion was completely alien to the old woman. 'Ore-bap, what have we done?' Nani cried out while holding her arms in the air. 'What do we do now?'

The feast went on, albeit more surreptitiously than initially planned. I ate the curried goat meat, too, but well out of my sister's sight. Tania ate her two minute noodles and green cordial, packed for the inevitable difficult eating days by my mother. Like a grieving widow she sat in the tin walled room with my grandmother, mother and other relatives offering their support.

Tania listened quietly, and wept briefly. She seemed relatively unaffected by it all, but when we got home she pronounced that she was a vegetarian, something she was able to maintain for three full months until her urge to eat cheeseburgers and super supreme pizzas overcame her.

4

Romantic Mismatch

I have never been able to see what my parents have in common. My mother is a highly social, anxious, literature obsessed woman who was raised to have a suspicion of both religion and money. She would quote from the great Bengali poet, Rabindranath Tagore, as she walked around the house, carrying dried fish and mango pickles to the kitchen.

'Let your life lightly dance on the edges of time like dew on the tip of a leaf,' she once said, before urging Tania and I never to experiment with drugs. I wasn't sure of the relevance.

'The dew is on the tip of the leaf, not eating or smoking it,' she told us on another occasion, fresh from a discussion about children and drugs with her Taxation Office colleagues. There she had acquired the nickname Queen Latifa.

My father was the prodigy from a dirt poor village called Bijoyrampur who was interested in matters practical – money, machines and charity. His skills were in mathematics and DIY handyman work. He seemed restless and unable to sit comfortably with company, either loitering around in the garden tilling the soil or fixing the carburettor in our decades old beige Toyota Corolla. When we walked together as a family he was often ten metres ahead of us, holding his hands behind his back. He seemed inaccessible, an advertisement for men as emotional islands.

I didn't see it as a problem. The message I had received from my parents and family friends while growing up was that, despite what the movies told us, romantic love was a dangerous modern concept, one that led to passion but was destined to end in tears.

'Yes, I married your father. Of course, love is a myth,' I remember my mother saying once.

With its flickering passions and fevers, romantic love was not the environment in which to raise children. Whether it occurred in a Bangladeshi village or within the British royal family, marriage was about renewing or elevating one's position on the social ladder, and then transmitting quality genetic code. I knew they were the views of the Old World, ones which my parents were struggling to maintain amid the assault of television, rock music and Coca-Cola.

But they were able to relent occasionally, relaxing their distrust of newfangled things, like the time they bought me an electric guitar for my sixteenth birthday when I was deep in the throes of a textbook teenage phase. I obsessed about Bon Jovi and randomly sang lines of 'Livin' On A Prayer'. The neighbours complained that the amplifier was too loud and I was consigned to the garage.

'Acha, please! Maths homework first, rock music later,' was my father's response, pointing me in the direction of my room.

My parents first met each other in the modest tin roofed house of my mother's parents in Dihi, which had been a part of East Pakistan since 1956. My father, Afsar, had a stellar reputation as a university academic in statistics. He was also fair skinned – 'forsha' in Bengali – which was highly prized. He was in his mid twenties and came with only a small entourage, unusual for a man of his billing. My mother's uncle, who was more of an interlocutor than Afsar's direct companion, was his lone attendant. The uncle was known as the 'ghatak', an agent of matrimony.

'Please, no bhaja food please,' Afsar began, lifting a palm as if to stop oncoming traffic, attempting to indicate his sophistication by communicating a distaste for fried food. 'I am very health conscious.'

The word quickly spread into the kitchen, where my grandmother was preparing furiously with a servant, stirring a pot over a fire, cooking a feast to please the potential suitor. 'Shudu shidho?' my grandmother said, confused about his desire for boiled food. 'Strange man.'

My mother, Minu, was the eldest daughter of the Khan family. She was sixteen years old and had just finished Year Ten at a Hindu boarding school, Mirzapur, even though she was from a Muslim family. She was one of the very few women in her region in the process of completing secondary studies. My grandfather didn't care for the Hindu background of the school, concerned only for its renowned reputation for producing bright, independent girls. But in spite of her exceptional education, a quality that had attracted her new suitor, she readied herself in a neighbouring room lacking crucial knowledge about the urgently important discipline of make-up and fashion.

'Ore-bap! Should I wear a necklace or earrings?' she asked her teenaged sister, Bulu, who was overseeing Minu's dressing. 'With my plain face he'll think I've just walked out of jail, or a funeral.'

After a period of dedicated attention during which the esteemed guest was met by my grandfather, his other children and curious neighbours, Minu strode in with her sister and greeted Afsar with the Islamic 'Salam alaykum', before taking a seat on the other side of the room on a wooden chair. From his seat on the bed, Afsar peered at her, leaning back slightly with his hands resting on the springy mattress, occasionally dusting his cream coloured shirt. He admired her red sari with the gold trim and noted the black bindi on her forehead with satisfaction.

'So, you will soon finish your schooling,' my father began. 'What subjects did you study for your Year Ten certificate?'

There was no pretence that marriage discussions were anything other than the most important job interview. My mother answered speedily that she studied history, English, economics and Bengali literature.

'Can you tell me the name of a famous economist?' my father asked matter-of-factly.

Minu was dumbstruck and looked around the room, making strained eye contact with her father and eldest brother, Badu. After a brief pause, her sister Bulu broke the silence by offering some sweets to Afsar.

'Tik ache,' said Afsar. 'No problem. Can you do the namaj?' he asked, assessing her religious credentials.

'Of course. Nischoi,' my mother squeaked, hoping to regain some ground. She knew how to pray, although she never did, unless somebody died. Her father didn't encourage Islamic religious practice among his children, focusing instead on a worldly education. But there was no way this ambivalence towards religion could be revealed now.

'I can read the Koran, too,' Minu added, lying through her teeth, desperately hoping that she wouldn't be asked to prove it.

'One more question, tik ache?' Afsar said.

Minu nodded anxiously.

'What is eight times seven?' he asked.

There was a brief pause while more nervous glances were exchanged between Minu and her family. Again, sweets were offered in desperation. Finally my mother feigned confidence, made direct eye contact with Afsar and offered her response.

'Fifty-four,' she said, her pulse quickening but without a bat from her eyelids.

There was an audible gasp in the room from the ghatak uncle and brother Badu. Afsar smiled and watched my mother go red as she realised her answer was wrong. Her eyes were downcast.

'It's OK. Abar – let's try again,' said my father, in an attempt to console. 'What is three times seven?'

'Twenty-one,' my mother answered promptly, with a slight tilt of her head. My father nodded, grinned and asked for a rasagullah sweet to celebrate.

Afsar left the household impressed with the display – both of the female on offer and the sophistication of the family – but not so overwhelmed by my mother's knowledge of economics and mathematics. He had already searched long and hard for a quality bride, but with little success. His qualifications meant he was in high demand and had even attracted the interests of a wealthy, city industrialist, eager to marry off his only daughter, only to baulk when he saw the meagre, deprived nature of my father's village and its inhabitants, living in mud huts without power or electricity.

On another occasion, my father had ventured to a neighbouring village to consider a possible candidate, only to find he was being ambushed. The girl's family had planned the event to begin as a simple meeting, but was to be upgraded at short notice to a full blown wedding if my father showed the remotest interest.

Within minutes of my father's arrival, the prospective fiancée arrived as a bride, dressed in a bright red sari and a garland of flowers around her neck. He was informed that the marriage would take place then and there, forcing my father to jump out through a window of the family's mud brick house and frantically run the several kilometres back home.

After meeting Minu, Afsar expressed his interest through the fixer uncle, but regretfully added that any marriage with her would have to wait because of an opportunity that arose for him in Karachi, the capital of Pakistan. It was the summer of 1969 and there was no Bangladesh. It was still called East Pakistan, the two territories split by the meandering mass of India.

'I have been offered a job at a prestigious insurance company in Karachi, Federal Life, with the promise of future study and a position in England. My bosses said I could go to the London School of Economics!' my father wrote to Minu, days before he boarded a Pakistan International Airways flight.

Afsar moved to the other end of his fragile, cobbled together country with three other colleagues – Jainal, Mrinal and Dhash. They were all studying to become actuaries, receiving course notes and directions from a centralised body based in London. My mother returned to the boarding school, Mirzapur, to complete the final years of her high schooling – Years Eleven and Twelve – with a view to attending university. The education system was built on the British model. There she would receive the occasional letter from my father, who signed off as an uncle to avoid arousing the suspicion of the college mistresses who disposed of any letters of a romantic nature.

Dear Minu,

I am settling into a flat with my housemates,
Mrinal, Dhash and Jainal. I try to cook for
them, but sometimes there is only the chapati
bread. Karachi is very hot and the people have
wide shoulders. I am applying probability ratios
to extract a good premium for the company.
Good luck in your studies.

Your uncle, Afsar.

My mother would diligently reply while she lay on her dormitory bed in the evening, scratching out her letters with an old fountain pen.

> Dear Afsar Uncle,
>
> The shapla flower floats in our pond and
> reminds me of nature's Beauty. It is there that
> I find my God. I feel the winter's breeze on
> my skin and think of Tagore's words: 'Beauty
> is truth's smile when she beholds her own face
> in a perfect mirror.' I hope to study English at
> Dhaka University next year.
>
> Your niece, Minu.

The backdrop to their innocent, burgeoning romance was growing political tumult. The Pakistani leaders in the west wanted to impose their language, Urdu, as the state language in the eastern territory, where the people spoke Bengali. As leverage, the government was denying the eastern territory crucial resources – money, food and arms. By now Afsar had spent a year in West Pakistan and was readying himself for a possible stint in London. Minu had finished her schooling and had gained entry to study English at the University of Dhaka. They continued to exchange letters but my father, not one to make hasty decisions that may have a financial impact, had not made any firm plans regarding a wedding.

With the two territories on the verge of war in early 1971, my father and his colleagues were told to return home immediately. Tanks rolled into the East, the military stormed key centres such as banks, water depots and government buildings, and the massacres began. Chaos ensued as everyone ran for cover, seeking safety in their home towns.

My mother returned to her village and family from her studies in Dhaka. Another brother, the last of the family's eight children, was born soon afterwards, his delivery occurring in broad daylight while gunfire could be heard in the background. He was named Bullet.

My mother and her younger sister, Bulu, were both likely targets for rape amid the disinhibited rage of their masters. If they went outside they dressed in a burqa, the only time in their lives that they ever wore the religious garment. If the soldiers came knocking, they lay under blankets.

'Please sir, leave them alone,' Minu's parents would say. 'They are sick old ladies trying to recover.'

Soon after my father returned home to Bijoyrampur, a list was made of the local intellectuals, professionals and industrialists who were then rounded up by the invading army generals. Those who could be found were lined up in the centre of town and maimed symbolically – the eye surgeon had his eyeballs poked out, the writer's hands were slit with a bayonet and the architect's limbs crushed with bricks.

Unknown to my father, his name had appeared on a similar list, but he found out fast enough when a family friend turned up in the dead of night to take him into hiding. They boarded a bus at dawn and he was smuggled into lodgings in the nearby town of Jessore. Afsar stayed there in virtual isolation for weeks, until one afternoon a neatly dressed, muscular soldier with a curly black moustache knocked loudly on his door and strode inside.

'So Mister, Bhaiya, your time has come!' he shouted in Urdu, revealing a shimmering bayonet atop a smoking rifle, freshly fired. 'You think you can hide forever?'

My father froze. Having worked in Karachi, he understood what the soldier was saying. As he raised his arms as if to surrender, a neighbour walked in to help him.

'Sir, please, he is not the traitor,' the balding, middle-aged man with a limp said, referring to the hastily arranged group of freedom fighters that was now resisting the military brutality. 'He is a good man and prays to Allah.'

The soldier stared at my father, momentarily relaxing his grip on the rifle. My father sensed his chance.

'I lived in Karachi for one year and worked in insurance. I hope to return. I am not a traitor and fear God the Almighty,' he said in fluent Urdu, taking the soldier by surprise.

A heavy silence ensued while the soldier locked eyes with his prey, then surveyed the bare single room dwelling. He lifted his rifle, then lunged at my father, pressing the sharp blade of the bayonet against his throat, turning it from side to side. My father closed his eyes, fearing his end.

'You were lucky this time, Bhaiya,' the soldier snarled. Then he charged out to battle once again. Catching the wind of his slim escape, my father hugged his neighbour in thanks.

Several months later, after almost three million people

had died, the war came to an abrupt end. The Indians joined the eastern territory in battle against the west to avert a mammoth refugee crisis on their border, just kilometres away from my mother's village. Their superior forces brought the Pakistanis to their knees within weeks.

Amid the death, rape and destruction a new country called Bangladesh was born. Radio Australia was the first English language service to announce it. A new leader, Sheikh Mujib, was hailed as the land's saviour. In 1972, the euphoria settled and famine arrived soon afterwards. The country was bankrupt and Henry Kissinger, the US Secretary of State, declared Bangladesh a basket case. But lives began afresh. My mother continued on with her first year of study at Dhaka University where she lived in a female dormitory and my father began a new job at an insurance company.

Frustrated by my father's matrimonial indecision, my mother's family found another suitor, a learned man living in Karachi. But when the end of the war grounded all flights to Bangladesh he was stranded, unable to return home. Having made no contact through the conflict, Afsar renewed his wedding proposal, but was met with resistance by his own immediate family who wanted a big dowry. Minu's father refused, offering only to pay for the gold and jewellery at the wedding. A row erupted and my father was caught in the peacetime crossfire, unable to appease his family. He visited my mother on the university campus, occasionally presenting her with a single rose bought at a nearby street stall.

Meanwhile, his family's attitude about the dowry ramped up. In their opinion, for such a rare find of a man, who had such humble beginnings – humble even for Bangladesh – a gargantuan payment was appropriate, mandatory almost. They demanded a motorcycle, several goats and cows, an allotment of land and a typewriter. The gold jewellery was a given.

It was a stalemate. There was a tense stand-off. The marriage looked doomed, until my father finally stepped in. 'I want to marry Minu,' he told his family, demanding that the metrics of the dowry payment be modified.

Finally they relented, realising the wheels of courtship had progressed too far to be thwarted. Minu and Afsar married weeks later in a simple ceremony without any fanfare in my mother's university dormitory room, her brother Badu carrying the wedding ring to the city from Dihi.

In spite of their pragmatic views about love and marriage, I can see now they had their own version of romance, one that was epic when seen in its context, almost thwarted by my father's indecision but ultimately saved by the end of a bloody war. There's a funny sort of destiny about them being together – the adventurous resilience they shared, which was forged in the chaos and instability of new nationhood, whetted their appetite for migration to a completely different country that could provide the safety, hope and opportunity they wanted for their children.

5
Traffic and Ties

'If you do anything like that again, I'll rip this tie off your neck,' said Dr Townsend sternly, tugging lightly on my black prefect's tie adorned with its golden badge.

'Yes, Sir. Sorry, Sir,' I replied, feeling the intimidating power of the headmaster's office, with its mahogany table and large, old paintings. It was like being a foreign leader scared into meekness by the grandeur of the White House.

I was in my final year of high school. The day before, while we waited for a lift after cricket training, a friend and I were throwing a tennis ball to each other over the top of the cars speeding by on New South Head Road, a busy highway in Sydney's eastern suburbs. We were wearing the school uniform, which included a blazer and a tie. It didn't feel dangerous, but there was the possibility of the ball hitting a car and perhaps enraging a member of the public.

Unluckily for us, one of the cars speeding by was a black Volvo that happened to be driven by our headmaster, Dr Townsend. He didn't immediately recognise us, but he carried out a thorough investigation that night by calling our coach and several other teachers at the sports ground. My friend received a warning, but I was singled out for special treatment because I was a prefect and on a full scholarship.

Dr Townsend had returned to Australia a few years earlier from a senior position at Eton College in the UK. He replaced Mr Mackerras, who had been the headmaster for decades and was a jolly man known for remembering everyone's name and handing out chocolate frogs. Townsend was a theology academic who had moved into teaching and education. He was a thin man with sleek spectacles and always dressed in black academic gowns. Although he was originally from Perth, it seemed his many years in England had thoroughly ingrained the cultural cringe into his views. 'There is more to life than sporting success, although you wouldn't know it in Australia,' he said during one of his first speeches to us in assembly after becoming the new headmaster. This was to a school where we were offered quantum physics as a leisure activity.

Initially thrilled when I had received a scholarship to Sydney Grammar, my father worried later that it might have been a mistake to send me there in case it encouraged me to look back in shame at my impoverished background. He also thought that the daily singing of hymns with strong Christian themes, the Latin classes and the compulsory attendance at rowing regattas were corrupting. It was more English than the English. In my first year, I didn't know a crotchet from a crowbar and came second last in my year in music. It was little consolation that I knew all the words to 'The Lord is my Shepherd'.

I felt equally uncomfortable when my father was the

only one drinking orange juice during toasts at important school functions or when our clumsy knife and fork technique was apparent during formal meals. I tried to practise at home with our handful of mismatched cutlery before major dinners but always had difficulty dissecting bony meat which seemed so much easier – and tastier – to eat with my hands. At home, that was how we always ate our rice and curry.

I'd already attended a dinner at our new headmaster's house, an old mansion by the harbour that seemed to have nothing other than bookshelf after bookshelf of academic journals and textbooks. I sat with the other prefects at a long formal table and tried to hide my fear of the shiny silver-plated implements in front of me. It was relaxed enough. I managed to sip the creamy orange pumpkin soup with the big spoon without incident and in spite of my fumbling with the knife and fork I was able to enjoy the main course – roast beef with a completely spice-free side of baked potatoes. I savoured the utter absence of chilli or turmeric. The food seemed naked. It was my version of porn.

In my first year at Grammar, my mother endured several sleepless nights when she was once asked to make a pasta salad following a cricket game by a parent of one of my team-mates. She had no idea what it was and sought advice from her work colleagues.

'What is this pasta salad, please?' she asked her boss at the debt collection department at the Taxation Office, where she still worked full-time. Her boss directed her to Woolworths and on the day of the cricket match she brought three completely different pasta salads, all neatly packed in styrofoam containers.

I learnt quickly that our relative wealth within the Bangladeshi community was laughable compared to that of some of my schoolmates. I stared agape at the first harbour-front home I visited for a birthday. In my first week at school I discovered what a Bentley was – one of the students used to get chauffeur driven in one. Once, when a school friend decided to visit our house unannounced, I kept him standing on our patio where I spoke to him for several minutes before saying goodbye. I was horrified at what he might have thought of our simple furnishings. We had no leather couches, no big screen TVs and certainly no pool table.

But my parents had also instilled in me a sense that Australians couldn't really look down on us like the British might. 'Their ancestors are all criminals, convicts,' my father said. 'We come from a culture of twenty thousand years. They do nothing but drink alcohol.' And so I inherited the uneasy tension of the class system in Australia.

I also quickly learnt that Grammar was still a meritocracy, an antipodean version of Eton. But unlike the institution of the British royal family, being rich wasn't in itself a marker of status if you were also dumb. Brains were given due respect and there was no need to feign stupidity in an effort to be more popular, like in primary school.

And being good at sport remained as high status as anywhere else in Australian society. I excelled in cricket and soccer, always being selected for the top teams. My father would drive me to the games and watch them from start to finish. I remember him beaming with pride and standing to applaud when I scored a fifty against a visiting cricket team from Brisbane Grammar. That day Greg Chappell was in the crowd cheering for his son, too.

It's difficult to know where my drive came from. Certainly, a huge emphasis on education seemed to be the norm in the Bangladeshi community. My family environment sheltered me from the more relaxed approach of my peers in primary school living in Toongabbie, who were taught there would always be a job of some sort. And if not, that didn't matter either because there was always the dole. I had also inherited a sense that if I didn't perform I might bring shame or dishonour on my parents, diminishing the sacrifices they made to bring me to Australia. In any case, my ongoing success helped me relax socially, and as I moved through the years of high school I became more mischievous, too. You could take the boy out of Toony, but you couldn't take Toony out of the boy. I had the bogan in me, too.

But even as a bogan there was a clear tension between me and my friends in western Sydney, who looked down on my private school links, and my posher friends at high school. As soon as I got off the train at Toongabbie, I'd shed as much as I could of my highly visible school uniform. Stepping out of my oversized grey blazer which, in my first year or so, hung down to my knees was a particular relief. My father had bought me a large one in the hope that it would last until my senior years but, of course, by then a series of growth spurts meant the blazer barely reached my waist and the school motto 'Laus Deo' – 'Praise to God' – had faded so much that it was barely legible. As soon as I walked in the door, I changed into my Parramatta Eels footy jersey and plotted out my activities for the afternoon. In Toongabbie, mischief made the man and there was something of a competition about who could perform the greatest acts of delinquency and get away with it. It's no wonder a portion of my suburban friends ended up in jail.

At school I was well behaved but enjoyed being the class clown and received two fatigues for bad behaviour, which is similar to detention, except that it includes some sort of repetitive activity, like conjugating Latin. I received one in Year Eight after I made reference to my maths teacher's penis on a note being passed around in class. In Year Nine I received another when my Latin textbook-cum-baseball bat sent a squash ball careering into my teacher's head. It was an accident, a little like manslaughter.

I also narrowly escaped being part of a mass expulsion of students after all hell broke loose at a party to celebrate the end of a musical production with a prestigious girls' school. The distant geography of my house saved me. I left early to make a train. But unproved allegations of drug use didn't stop five friends getting the boot.

In my final two years, I befriended a tall guy called Daniel, a new pupil from the south west of Sydney. I noticed him after he beat me in a chemistry test. I picked him for my team in a game of soccer based entirely on his slavic roots, only to see an ill-timed kick of his, as goalie, miss the ball completely and watch it roll between his legs and into the net. Like me, he had a thirst for mischief and a chip on his shoulder inherited from the ethnic western Sydney experience. He once stole another pupil's sunglasses by breaking into his BMW, which was parked in the playground, with some kind of packaging tape, much to the astonishment and admiration of our peers. He folded it up like origami, slid it between the closed doors and then created a loop on the end with which he flicked the lock.

But the tennis ball-throwing incident that I was now being hauled up in front of Dr Townsend for was more consistent with other traffic related offences I had already notched up in Toongabbie. I feared the nature of any upcoming punishments. If I'd been with my neighbourhood friends, I would have been lauded as a legend.

For my most memorable feat, there had been least six of us, most of them guys I barely knew. After Lynchy left for the north coast, my best friend became Fazil, whose dad ran the mobile Turkish kebab van. We played tennis together most afternoons and he loved showing off his Reebok runners and his Adidas tracksuit pants. Sometimes I'd tag along with his friends from school, Pendle Hill High, or 'Pendo'. I often pretended I went to Pendo, too, swearing along with the best of them.

There was Pete, who sported a rats-tail and an AC/DC T-shirt and who, annoyingly, kept getting me mixed up with Raj, a Fijian kid who obsessively collected footy cards. The other two were freckled white guys who kept quoting from the TV show *Growing Pains*, usually making references to having a boner.

That day, we crouched like hidden assassins behind a set of large pine trees that were on an embankment next to a busy street, Fitzwilliam Road. Each of us was carrying four or five water bombs. Cars were driving past at seventy and eighty kilometres an hour and our logic was that, at those speeds, the drivers would have little interest in stopping or coming after us if we pelted them.

The plan worked for the first three or four cars. We received several angry honks, one man unwinding his window to present an upright middle finger and another driver who yelled out, 'Ya fuckin' bloody Abos!' He'd probably noticed my dark skin, as well Raj's. It only encouraged us further.

When a black four-wheel drive headed towards us the entire group took aim with our remaining water bombs and struck the car in several different places as it whooshed past. The noise of the balloons colliding all at once was like a sonic boom. I remember seeing several people rushing out of the nearby fibro houses to see what had happened. We gave each other high fives and debated whether the last attack was the most satisfying.

'Oh man, that was cool,' said Fazil, putting his palm in the air in expectation of a high five from me. I missed the cue.

'I've got a boner from that, guys,' said one of the freck-led guys, before laughing hysterically.

Suddenly there was a screech of brakes as the four-wheel drive came to halt a hundred metres away. Then the driver did a sharp U-turn and sped back toward us. We could all see the man behind the wheel, a stocky dad wearing a rugby jumper with his wife in the front seat and his two children in the back. I made fleeting eye contact. His teeth were clenched and he motioned with a wave of his fist that he was coming to get us. In unison, a rush of panic-stricken expletives rang out from our group.

'Fuuuckenshiiit!' we chorused in a grand, unified swear word. Then, again simultaneously: 'Run!'

I felt a massive rush of adrenaline and sprinted to a nearby alleyway. I turned into it at such speed that I careered into the wooden fence on one side. It didn't seem to slow me down. I just kept running, grateful that I was a member of the Grammar athletics team and one of the fastest sprinters in my year. I tore past an elderly woman walking with a cane before turning toward another street that split into several small lanes. It was only then that I looked back to see Fazil only a few metres behind me, his arms pumping like pistons.

We had lost all of our other fellow water bombers. When the fear of life and death hit, it was every boy for himself. After walking together for almost half an hour through obscure streets, Fazil and I finally headed to our respective homes knowing we had only just escaped disaster.

'Phew. That was close,' I said, pleased with myself.

'That guy looked really pissed off,' said Fazil, before parting ways.

As I walked toward my house, I saw a police car reverse out of the driveway. My heart skipped a beat. My initial thought was that we had been robbed. My parents were waiting on the small patio. They looked mortified, like someone had died. Amma's head was bowed and Dad was breathing heavily. Then he started growling and motioned for me to come immediately. Amma sensed his anger and grabbed him on the arm, pleading that he remain calm.

'A friend of yours said you threw something at a car and almost injured small children!' my father yelled in Bengali. 'Police came here, into our house, asking questions about you!'

I looked at him, confused, but had little chance for a right of reply.

'Baba, a boy brought the driver and police to our house and said you were the leader,' my mother said in a more conciliatory, sympathetic tone. 'His name was Peter.'

That prick, I thought to myself. He barely knew my name. He probably thought he was going to Raj's house.

My father grabbed me by the ear and dragged me to my room, demanding that I perform the ear and squat punishment, reserved for my most shameful disciplinary breaches. I hadn't done it for years, not since I was caught sticking a sausage into the exhaust pipe of a primary school teacher's car.

'Kan dhor,' he said, which was a command to grab my ear lobes, the punishment of choice in Bangladesh's public schools. I imagined university education lecturers instructing aspiring teachers how to carry out the punishment, perhaps aided by drawings of children like me assuming the pose.

While my father saw it as a humiliation, I was just glad to avoid a thorough beating. The ear–squat punishment was the equivalent of doing community service instead of a jail term. I gripped my ear lobes before squatting up and down fifty times, counting each one in Bengali.

Back in Dr Townsend's mahogany room of awe, the episode flashed into my mind. I stood erect and still like a soldier, silent and staring at the headmaster as he held my tie. For a few brief seconds I couldn't hear what he was saying. His voice seemed so far away. And I could feel my body beginning to follow an ancient code, a reflex I seemed to have no control over. I grabbed my earlobes and began to squat.

'What on earth are you doing, young man?' Dr Townsend barked, incredulous, his face scrunched up in a look of shock. 'Have you lost your mind?'

I regained my senses. Mortified and fearing imminent expulsion, I told him something, anything – perhaps that it was an exercise my doctor had asked me to repeat several times a day. Then I apologised profusely and scurried out of the office, assuring him that neither activity would ever happen again – the squat or the throwing of objects at cars.

And they never did, in part because my enthusiasm for mischief began to wane the more I grew apart from my Toongabbie friends. But I often think the punishment could be successfully rebranded as some kind of exercise routine, like Zumba or Tae Bo.

6

Love, God and Dissection

I fell for my first love dissecting a rat. The frozen animals were handed out to share between two. We laid it on its back and pinned it down with its fore and hind legs splayed outwards on the cutting board. I stared at it briefly, momentarily giving thanks to the animal sacrificing its body upon the altar of medical science before admiring my partner's shiny black hair. We cut open its thin, white hairy body with scissors and sliced open the layer of skin that encased its digestive system – floppy, rubbery bits of bowel, a thin, pink, shiny tube of oesophagus and a cute, oval shaped stomach.

It was my first semester of university. I had chosen Sydney University to study Medicine. The decision wasn't made with any great inspiration or commitment, but mostly because I'd achieved the entrance mark to get in. I was eighteen years old. I had no idea what I wanted to do with my life. Several of my friends from high school, like Daniel, had also chosen the course. It seemed like a good idea at the time.

My biology partner was a girl called Sheree. She was short, flicked her hair around a lot and wore colourful, floral dresses. She smelled great, like Chanel perfume. She was raised in Australia but her parents were Chinese–Singaporean. I thought of her when I watched ads for Singapore Airlines on TV. She could be my very own Singapore girl.

'I think doing medicine builds good character,' Sheree told me soon after we first met. Her father was a renowned surgeon.

I thought about the role models in my life. None of them had been doctors. My father said he wished I was studying to become an actuary like him, then we could run a family owned insurance company together. That probably would have built character, too, but it didn't appeal.

By the end of my first month I had already been rejected by a gothic looking girl. To expand my social horizons, I began an arts degree in parallel, studying anthropology and politics. I didn't have any great intellectual interest in either at the time, but thought I might meet interesting people. Her name was Bridget and she wore a nose ring and liked alternative music. She was raven-haired, had porcelain skin, carried a backpack and always wore black. I pretended to like The Cruel Sea to attract her interest and read up on its lead singer, Tex Perkins. I wanted to be a goth, too, but my skin was too dark.

Bridget humoured me briefly by agreeing to watch a movie with me one night. A week later at a university concert, I met her new love interest, a long-haired rocker with tattoos of a snake on his shoulder. I'd been preparing to dazzle her with my knowledge of punk rock band Weezer and felt defeated, put in my place as an Indian looking medical nerd. I had flirted with coolness and failed.

I returned to my medical brethren with my tail between my legs. At least they were more like me – studious types, usually ethnic and finally ready to let their hair down. Sheree and I bonded further, chatting as we lay on the grass on campus. In class we'd progressed to the dissection of a frog, which we electrocuted to watch its leg muscles contract and illustrate our knowledge gained from physiology classes. I continued to experiment with subcultures and Sheree and I attended various meetings of clubs and groups – Indian dance parties, Chinese Christian lunch meetings and our very own booze fests, which were sponsored by pharmaceutical companies. I even joined the Mediaeval Society, dressing up once as an archer for a mock recreation of the Battle of Hastings.

University social life seemed divided along ethnic lines. The white people did arts degrees and hung around Manning House where they watched theatre sports and listened to rock music, attending their obligatory two or three lectures a week in between. Most of the Asians studied technical courses like science or economics and loitered in the cafeteria in the Wentworth Building. We joked that the wogs – the Lebanese, Italians and Greeks – spent all their days in the bar there. Daniel and I once saw a brawl unfold between a couple of Lebanese and Turkish guys over who invented the doner kebab.

'Fuck off, Rashid, there's no way Lebs could have come up with that!' yelled a muscular guy called Orhan. Clearly the rotating, kebab heating machine was one of civilisation's greatest gifts. 'They just flogged it off us and sold the parts. All you guys have ever come up with are car stereos that are bigger than your cars.'

One of our medical student friends, Ali, always skipped lectures and virtually lived at Wentworth Bar. Like many of his Lebanese mates, he claimed he was part French. 'You know I'm French–Lebanese,' he'd tell us, flashing his fancy MX-5 keyring. 'Bonjour. Ca va. Wallah,' he said. Daniel and I joked that the Lebanese guys would always use the word 'wallah', which means 'I promise in the name of God', when they were stretching the truth. Ali dreamt of becoming an astronaut. If that failed, he wanted to be a pilot so he could fly over the beach at Brighton Le Sands where his other Lebanese friends hung around.

'So why are you doing Medicine?' I asked him one day.

'Oh, it's just a fall-back,' he replied, giggling.

As my first year sped past, I flirted with different subcontinental groups. There was the Tamil Society, the Indian Association and a Pakistani friendship group. I liked that, as expatriates, partition didn't matter. We were virtually all the same. We ate curry, were crazy about cricket and worried that our parents might try and arrange marriages for us. I had dream Indian credentials – I was studying to become a doctor and was good at cricket – but I just couldn't come at pretending to be African American and adopting the theatre of hip-hop, which was what many of the guys seemed to revert to in expressing their cultural difference. I couldn't understand how thin, Indian guys studying economics or engineering could consider themselves big, tough and well endowed. From my encounters in male change rooms most guys of Asian origin, myself included, were usually short and thin in more ways than one. I was pretty sure that the various rumours about black guys did not extend to South Asians.

Sheree and I first kissed at an afterparty of the year's Medical Revue. That year it was called the Dead Patient's Society. She was one of the main singers and I was in a group of guys acting like the Jackson Five. 'You're here not for your singing ability, but because you're dark-skinned, all right?' the producer told us during our first rehearsal. We weren't allowed to sing but just clicked our fingers over a backing track of 'Blame it on the Boogie'.

The party was at the parents' house of one of the revue directors, a sandstone mansion on Sydney's lower North Shore. Later that night we snuck off to a rock formation overlooking a bay where we sealed our burgeoning romance with a lingering kiss. We were both first born overachievers who shared a love of bad eighties music and seafood laksa.

Our relationship arose among a trend of many guys having Asian girlfriends. A joke that there was yellow fever on campus was doing the rounds. Opinions on the reasons for their popularity varied from their soft, sensuous skin, a propensity for youthful looks, their sheer numbers on campus and even their apparent performance in the bedroom.

'You know they're screamers, don't you?' Daniel informed me days after I announced Sheree and I were an item. I didn't know, but I longed to find out.

Long before the idea of ChinIndia arose, encapsulating the dual economic rise of China and India, Daniel labelled the growing trend of Indian guys with Asian girls as the Curry-bug Combo, like it was a McDonald's meal. The curry part didn't require explanation, but Daniel referred to Asians on campus as bugs because many wore thick glasses and existed in large numbers. 'They're just swarming the place, bro,' he told me. I laughed uncomfortably.

I was encountering a lot of racism against my new girl-friend. Even my own mother hid her disappointment when I revealed Sheree as a love interest. While the future doctor part was a plus, the Asian bit was not. Bangladeshis in our community often referred to Asians perjoratively as 'nak-bocha', which means flat-nosed. The general rationale was that ethnic groups could be as racist as they liked, but if a white person made similar comments they'd be pilloried as hate-mongering Nazis.

Our relationship seemed to be travelling fine until one rainy night in her room. 'I just don't think there is any point in going on,' Sheree told me. 'You're not a Christian.'

Somehow, without any warning, God had infiltrated my love life. Sheree wasn't even religious from what I could see, but she wanted to be. She was a bit like my father.

'It ended before it started,' Daniel laughed the following day, before realising he should be more sensitive. 'But don't worry, man. There's chicks everywhere.'

It was probably just an excuse to get rid of me. There's no comeback to breaking up because of religion. My heart was broken. It mended in due course, but for the next year our relationship entered an on-again, off-again stage. In an episode of his show, Jerry Seinfeld said that breaking up was like pulling the stringy bits of cheese off a slice of pizza. I knew exactly what he meant. The long, slow process of romantic disentangling was draining. Sheree's constant proximity meant it was difficult to cut ties and I struggled to become interested in other girls.

Meanwhile, the juggernaut of Medicine continued. I learnt the Krebs Cycle in biochemistry, how genes replicate themselves in our cells by a kind of biological photocopying and how the concentration of salts affect the way that our heart muscle contracts. The week before our first year examinations, Daniel and I studied together frantically at the warehouse of his father's Bobcat hire company, drinking guarana to stay up all night. During the actual exams I suffered its diuretic after-effects and had to keep running out to use the bathroom. By then I'd given up on university groups and societies, deciding that Medicine was enough of a club. I remained diligent, but not inspired.

Meanwhile, Sheree tried to interest me in Christianity, asking me to attend her church, where I drank the red wine, symbolizing the blood of Christ. I even read verses of the Bible and tried to argue with her about them.

'C'mon. It says one thing in Deuteronomy and something completely different in Revelations,' I said one night as we studied together.

'You can't take it literally,' she countered enigmatically. I rolled my eyes.

I was never going to convert to Christianity. While I

was born a Muslim, my family was very secular, particularly my mother who viewed Islam as an impediment to the flourishing of the arts and literature which she loved.

As Sheree and I migrated to different social groups and our studies moved us away from campus and to laboratories and hospitals, our relationship slowly dissipated. Dissection had graduated to human bodies, where we cut up emaciated corpses smelling of formalin. They were rumoured to be beggars from India, forgotten people whose bodies could be sold off. It was more confronting than the rats, especially if their dead, stony eyes were left open.

Some of the girls threw around dissected penises like they were pieces of meat and were met with shrieks from the guys, while also cradling uteruses like they were their own children. As I dutifully cut up organs and muscles there were no further sparks of romance, only revelry and revulsion in equal parts. When bowels had to be opened up and the faeces cleaned out to reveal the lining of the intestines, I routinely found myself gagging.

By the end of my second year, I was beginning to feel dejected about my realities not living up to my expectations. The true nature of a medical career dealing with body bits and odours was a real comedown, as was my failure in forming any lasting relationships.

While it was still early days, it was perhaps then I started to wonder about what it might be like to be a psychiatrist.

7

The Other Taliban

It was Eid day, the celebration that caps off Ramadan. I sometimes referred to as 'Ram it Down' due to the heavy feasting that goes on before sunrise and after sunset to compensate for the fasting during daylight.

My father and I were sitting cross-legged on a hard wooden floor, watching the steady arrival of latecomers as they took their shoes off at the door, nodding our heads in greeting to those we knew.

We were sitting in the assembly hall of a primary school in Matraville, one of the areas in Sydney with a large population of Bangladeshis. Neighbouring suburbs Hillsdale and Maroubra were the same, favoured for their proximity to the airport for the many taxi drivers in the community. Bleary-eyed from waking at dawn and then commuting for an hour to make it in time for the seven o'clock prayer, I was already nodding off.

I was in my early twenties. Halfway through my medical studies, I still lived at home. Abba and I wore matching grey panjabis. I received a new one every year in what was, for me, the world's most predictable gift. I had also donned my prayer hat. Mine looked like a white shower cap made of cotton, bulging outwards from my head. Our identical brown leather Bata sandals, bought on return trips to the homeland, were neatly arranged by the entrance with the rapidly extending lines of other shoes – thongs, leather lace-ups and sneakers.

My mother and sister weren't attending the prayer, preferring to stay at home instead and prepare the gargantuan quantities of food required for the steady procession of guests and the extreme eating that would take place throughout the day. When they did attend, they sat with the women in a cordoned-off section toward the back of the hall, something that annoyed them greatly. They were part of a silent minority for whom religious observance was a show. 'The only time I wore a burqa was in war time,' my mother bragged on numerous occasions.

The very first Sydney Bangladeshi community cricket tournament was starting in a few weeks and I and a group of my friends were determined to be a part of it. We had planned a training session after the prayer. From my place next to my father, I watched the cramped hall fill to overflowing as an influx of taxi drivers, their night shifts over, filed into the hall. They arrived in their blue uniforms and prayer hats before nonchalantly walking to the back of the hall where there was still some space. I could see some of my friends beginning to arrive.

Shahan, the just-graduated lawyer who lived within walking distance, arrived wearing expensive sneakers which he dutifully removed and left outside. He strolled into the hall with a fresh short back and sides haircut from the day before, and was dressed in a regal blue panjabi. The whites of his cricket pants were visible underneath. Practice or not, Shahan believed he played better when he wore white. Shahan and I had become close after high school. He'd also attended an expensive private school and often talked about the challenge of balancing what he called his 'white world' of posh school friends and girls with his Bangladeshi and Muslim worlds.

Given that my mother grew up in a family that was suspicious of Islam and religion in general, my own background is quite secular. Amma's parents had watched partition up close and the ensuing bloodshed between Hindus and Muslims. They also resented Muslims criticising the music, dance and culture that was so precious to their way of life. It scarred them forever, a trauma and resentment that was transmitted to my mother and her siblings, my uncles and aunties. However, I was still circumcised, we never consumed pork or alcohol at home and we attended mosque during funerals and holy days, much like the average atheist Christian.

My father is not particularly religious, but his parents were very devout Muslims. Like Marx, he thought religion was useful for the poor. He hoped that my sister and I would embrace Islam a little, believing that the discipline might shield us from social excesses.

I was attracted to the sense of belonging that came with praying with others in a mosque or from eating from the same bowl, but I felt I didn't entirely belong anywhere –

at school I was an impoverished Westie and in my own neighbourhood I was a private school snob. Even at university I wasn't all that interested in my degree, only barely interested in medicine as a career. I'd tried every subculture under the sun, from the chess club to my one week as an army cadet at high school. I'd even hung around with some beach loving surfie types from my Grammar cricket team. I couldn't swim but I could quote from the movie *Point Break*. I realised then that subcultures don't mix easily – or at the very least, being a dark-skinned Asian surfie who couldn't surf was unlikely to be a successful incarnation of myself.

There was a piece of me that wanted to be religious so I could experience the intense emotions and tight unity. Given Muslims aren't meant to drink, taking part in a prayer session is basically like going to the pub. The only problem was that I didn't believe in God; I still don't. I also quite enjoy alcohol and bacon. These are significant obstacles.

I always feel like a complete fraud in the setting of prayer, so much so that I call myself the Dodgy Muslim. I'm much more comfortable in a Christian church where it's accepted that at least some of the people attending don't believe in God. But growing up in a traditional community where religious observance was still the norm, my lack of engagement was obvious, to me at least. In the days leading up to that Eid day, I had barely fasted. In fact, I had invented my own fast where, instead of waking pre-dawn to eat a meal, I'd woken up at my normal time, enjoyed a large breakfast and then attempted to fast. I still drank water, but just tried to avoid eating. I basically just skipped lunch.

I had also forgotten a lot of the words used in prayer and found myself murmuring random nothings to maintain appearances. When I did know the words I'd recite them loudly, like singing the chorus of a song with great gusto when you don't know the lyrics to the verses. Praying for me was like doing karaoke or singing in the car, the crowd in the assembly hall hiding my ineptitude.

The imam who led the prayer was the same guy who had taught me Arabic as a child at Sunday school. The imam was an overweight man with a trimmed black beard. He was from Palestine and often made references to the evil Jewish conspiracy that ruled the world with the blessing of the Americans. He used to whack me on the knuckles if I recited Koranic verses wrongly. He held a deep animosity to anything he classified as Western. He berated us when we played tricks on each other during April Fool's Day or brought eggs at Easter. I once received a slap on my hand with a ruler after telling him that I had painted my face white, dressed up as a ghost and went trick-or-treating on Halloween.

But he had a good heart underneath, often giving me hugs and wishing my family the best. That morning he led the prayer, first lifting up his palms and reciting three Allahu-Akbars, slowly pronouncing the words with the correct Arabic diction, which always sounded to me as if he had a frog in his throat. He was dressed in a bright green tunic and wore a golden turban, and as he continued the prayer he held his arms aloft, like an eagle in flight. His grandeur was interrupted by the shrieks and distortion of a stuttering old microphone system. Like a low-energy aerobics class, the congregation stood as one and we followed his actions, bending, touching our foreheads to the floor and then standing again.

Once it was over, we had our special holy day hug, embracing each other and moving our heads from shoulder to shoulder. It's like the European kiss on each cheek, except there's no kissing, only hugging. Some men were particularly enthusiastic, performing the embrace at lightning speed, barely acknowledging each person before they moved on to another. It seemed like cheap, religious loving, as if collecting greetings was a good deed in itself.

Like me, a number of my friends were behaving like prayer hussies that morning, eager to get to the cricket. We hugged each other, said brother a lot, in combination with mate, and then smoked cigarettes out the front, dressed in our panjabis. Most of us didn't even smoke but made an exemption for special gatherings such as Eid. Considering the devout couldn't drink at bars, it was the only available chemical vice. While we stood together on the patio outside, cars honked as they passed, seeming to acknowledge our carnival atmosphere while they commuted to work.

Soon afterwards, we left our fathers for our game of cricket at Maroubra beach, the less glamorous strip of Sydney sand known for the Bra Boys and its housing commission estates. Still dressed in our robes, prayer hats and loose baggy pants, nine of us batted a gaffer-taped tennis ball around the deserted beach. The occasional jogger or early morning surfer watched with great curiosity, the sound of waves crashing in parallel with the whack of the tennis ball.

Our haphazard team had existed for years, since my late teens. We'd been meeting regularly on the weekends to play cricket in the car park of a Matraville supermarket, initially during Bangladeshi community functions and later, when we could drive, on our own. We were all kids from the Bangladeshi community but from different parts of Sydney. Ash and Ray came with me from the west; the others were all easties. Ash was short for Ashfaq, but lots of kids would predictably tease him and call him Ashfuck. He had to keep saying his name sounded like 'Ashfar' with an r, but in frustration eventually just abbreviated it to Ash. I'd known him since we'd arrived in Australia. Our families often met on the weekends.

Ray's full name was Anirban Habib Razzaque, but somehow it just became Ray. He had arrived from America when he was thirteen and paraded the whole homeboy look – big cap on backwards, a love of rap music and lots of references to 'dude' and 'man'. He couldn't really play cricket and held the bat aloft like he was playing baseball, but we brought him along anyway. His father had fled Bangladesh when the first president, Sheikh Mujib, was assassinated. Ray's father was a devoted supporter of Mujib's party, the Awami League, and was in fear for his life when his idol was killed. In Australia he headed up an association devoted to his hero, running events and meetings in the western suburbs and occasionally bickering with other Bangladeshi elders who set up opposing organisations.

Ash, Ray and I would meet up with the Bangladeshi kids living in the eastern suburbs. They lived in the poorer parts like Matraville or Eastlakes but were snobby about it, making fun of us for living so far away. It was an early lesson that status in Sydney depended on real estate. You could live in a dump, but if it was an eastern suburbs dump you could still hold your head high. They referred to the western suburbs like it was another country, a kind of far off bogan desert where every second house was a burnt down fibro shack and marauding criminals roamed the streets.

Our friendships were limited by geography but every couple of months we'd been meeting to play cricket and as the first tournament approached we ramped it up to more regular meetings. We used our games to escape the monotony of Bangladeshi community functions with their endless Indian style dancing or the seemingly infinite number of Bengali songs sung over and over, accompanied by a harmonium, which is a bit like a piano accordion. My mother sometimes sang. My father, a devoted community man, often helped organise the functions and held bureaucratic titles such as Assistant Vice President or First Treasury Secretary of the Bangladesh Association of New South Wales. Back then the community was small and they met regularly to remember the language and culture they had left behind, one that millions of people had died to protect.

We were just boys who didn't understand any of that and preferred to play cricket. In the carpark of the Matraville

Coles, we used a large green bin for the stumps and the trolley bay as the marker for one of the boundaries. If we couldn't get there, we'd set up a cricket game in the corridor of a house, or a garage or a community hall, depending on the function. There was almost no place where a spontaneous game of cricket could not be manufactured.

Shahan, my wise-cracking lawyer friend, was our designated captain. His older, lankier brother Omar was there, too. Faisal was the eldest and the senior statesman of the team. He was a tall, fair guy who was the most devout among us. A talented mathematician, he later left a potentially lucrative career in finance because Islam forbade usury. He was something of a religious mentor for another member of the team, Pushkin, who was a stocky grunge music enthusiast. He was also addicted to Coca-Cola and, at his peak, drank a couple of litres a day.

The other members included Moz, who was also a brilliant mathematician and the only left-hander in the team. A softly spoken metrosexual who brought skin moisturiser to the games, Moz was known for having the most expensive gear and accessories. He once told me that he admired my father and it was one of the reasons he was studying to be an actuary.

There was also Mitz, a slightly erratic young guy who wore an earring. Mitz's father was known in the community as the Bangladeshi Captain Cook, widely regarded as the first person from the region to set foot in Australia after he fell in love with an Australian aid worker and followed her home. This was in the mid 1960s, before Bangladesh was even formed. The relationship failed and Mitz's father returned to Bangladesh to marry and brought his new wife to Sydney, a union that would later produce Mitz.

In 1998 we decided to call our cricket team The Taliban. It came from the strong religious dimension within our group of friends, even if some of us didn't subscribe to it entirely. Faisal was the key advocate for the name. The word meant 'student' in Arabic and seemed to fit with our life stage as idealistic young adults who felt a little different from the white, Anglo mainstream. Being Muslim meant more than just the religion. I identified as being part of a large group of people that stretched from Africa to North America and one that was often disenfranchised and beaten down by powerful oppressors, or so I believed at the time. We also got to wear fashionable hats with inscriptions of prayers in fancy calligraphy or frilly ribbons hanging from them like a tail. We'd even come up with a celebration ritual for the team, pretending to fire Kalashnikovs into the air.

In my early years at university, I watched Faisal and Pushkin become very religious. They grew beards, refused to enter bars or nightclubs and even visited a sheikh regularly in Egypt. They were known as the hardcore Muzzos. I attended dinners with them where the seating was organised so that no male sat next to a woman who wasn't their partner. Soon after graduating from university, Faisal married the daughter of a well-known wedding photographer in an arranged marriage.

Moz and Shahan were also religious, but their practice was more relaxed. They had lots of friends who weren't

Muslim and didn't mind meeting them in bars, watching them drink alcohol while they sipped on soft drinks all night. I once took part in a drinking game with Shahan where he drank Coke instead of beer and he appeared more drunk than anybody else by the end of the night. He was dancing alone in the closet.

The tournament began two weeks after our initial beach training session, and the other teams and their members were a great barometer of the different sections of the local Bangladeshi community. They ranged from a team of recent high school graduates dominated by accounting students who were called The Young All Stars to an older team recruited from kitchen staff working at the multitude of Indian restaurants in Sydney called The Brothers. During one of the games I overheard some of the members of The Brothers pining for their halcyon business days of two decades before, when the word 'multicultural' meant they could charge fifteen dollars for dahl, essentially boiled lentils, to rapturous praise from the Aussie locals.

There were also The M2 Spinners, mostly family friends aged in their forties, named for the proximity of their households to the new freeway carved through the western suburbs. The youngest team was a ragtag bunch of high school students and rebel wannabes who called themselves The East Hills Gunners. Sporting crewcuts and bandannas, they wanted to put the bad in Bangla but unfortunately for them, after aping their favourite rappers about killing cops and conquering hordes of fawning women, they often had to run home to do their maths homework.

When the action turned to the game itself, our team dominated and we went on to win the competition three years in a row. While the Afghan Taliban relied on Toyota Land Cruisers and satellite phones for the advantage, ours relied on the many years of high quality cricket coaching within Australian high schools.

The finals in each tournament attracted large audiences from within the local community and were completed with formal presentations, which included a speech from my father as head of the organising committee. My mother would attend the finals with her friend Rama, but rarely knew what was happening, too busy sharing gossip and pre-cooked food with her friend in the stands. While we were awarded a level of prestige from our victories and our continued domination of the tournament, we were also widely loathed for our name and a certain perceived arrogance. Being raised in Australia, we brushed it aside as a form of inherited tall poppy syndrome.

When the tournament was on, Shahan and I spent hours debating team strategy. Although he talked about its challenges, I admired Shahan's ability to find a balance between his religion and his wider life without them becoming diametrically opposed. His father was a well known Islamic scholar and had written a book chronicling the varieties of Islamic names and their meanings. If it reflected popularity, half the book would have read 'Mohammed'.

As I'd discovered in my first year in Medicine, it was necessary to keep our love lives hush-hush. Almost every one of us had had girlfriends at some stage at university, which we usually maintained in secret from our parents. We would introduce them as friends or 'study partners'. The girls were rarely invited to the family home. Nights spent together were sold as needing to stay with a friend after a late night out in the city. Any prospect of getting serious was usually preceded by a conversation about converting to Islam.

Pushkin had a Portugese girlfriend for almost five years and only introduced her to his parents just before they were married. His girlfriend's parents demanded a separate function where they could drink alcohol. Shahan's relationship with a Jewish girl was heralded at university as a kind of roadmap to the resolution of the Middle East crisis. They broke up eventually citing their religious differences.

But the backdrop of our personal dramas of love, university life and emerging careers was the cricket team. Just before the fourth year of the tournament, the World Trade Centre in New York was attacked. Like the cliché that people remember where they were when JFK was assassinated, I remember being in a hospital dorm room with two other doctors, having eaten two minute noodles after drinking at a local bar.

I opened up my email account some time on the following day to find over twenty messages from the cricket team members. They varied from Shahan accusing Faisal of being a pilot under consideration to fly the planes to an emerging debate about whether our name was still suitable given the new circumstances. One of our team-mates, Moz, was in New York when it happened, having been sent there for a training course at a Wall Street bank.

The issue was that we had already entered our team as The Taliban in the upcoming tournament. It had been scheduled to begin a month later and a host of paperwork had been sent for approval to local authorities to confirm the use of grounds and umpires. A couple of weeks later my father received a letter from the local migrant resource centre, a government funded community group that helped link migrants to local services, asking him to explain the nature of one of the teams on the competition sheet. The centre didn't have any dealings with the tournament but the Chair of the centre was curious as to whether there was anything untoward about our cricket team.

My father sent back a simple message saying that the name was merely a joke among some silly young boys, not mentioning of course that one of those silly young boys was his own son. He also suggested he was sure the name would be changed in the wake of recent international events.

We had a team meeting soon afterwards. It was a heated, argumentative gathering in Moz's city apartment. I didn't want to be associated with the name – the connotation was too tainted, even if its use was in a tiny suburban cricket competition. 'We'd have eggs on our faces professionally if it ever became known,' I said.

Shahan's brother, Omar, said that colleagues at his accounting firm were joking about his name's resemblance to the Taliban leader. 'They call me Mullah Omar at Friday night drinks,' he added. The last thing he needed was to be associated with a bona fide Taliban group.

Faisal was adamant that the name could be maintained but he was howled down and finally relented, allowing debate on possible new names. It felt like a formal meeting of state, as if an important cabinet decision was being made. The team's carefree genesis in the carpark of a deserted Coles seemed a distant memory.

'How about Al-Qaeda?' Faisal said, emitting a brief giggle.

'You're only half joking, too,' Shahan retorted. 'Uh, I don't think so.'

Other suggestions varied from Sonar Bangla, which means Golden Bengal, to Habibis, which is 'darlings' in Arabic. The ultimate winner was Saracens, suggested by Moz and Pushkin, the name of the Islamic warriors from Spain who conquered all in their path almost a millennium ago. They were renowned for their sophistication in mathematics and the sciences, a fact that had been repeatedly shoved down my throat in Arabic Sunday school. Then we took an anonymous vote. We all wrote the name we wanted on a piece of paper.

Having grown more apathetic as the night went on, I voted for Saracens, too, feeling it was so obscure that nobody would understand the reference anyway. I felt removed from the themes of Muslim defiance that the choice of team names symbolised and I was also aware that some of the things the terrorists and Al-Qaeda operatives were saying weren't so different to some of the statements I had heard from those around me all my life. Things like the importance of the ummah, or the global Islamic community, and how it trumped any national identity, as well the gripe that we Muslims from South Asia, like the Arabs, had been humiliated by Western powers. I was uncomfortable about linking myself to the Arab world just by virtue of being born a Muslim. I didn't feel I had much in common with the Middle East. Its food was bland. Its language sounded rough to me and the garb it demanded suited a desert climate.

But Saracens it was. The first few games were spent trying to explain to our opponents, friends and family what the hell the Saracens were.

'They were these Islamic warriors when Spain used to rule all of Europe.'

'The rule of the Saracens was the last time Muslims dominated anybody else.'

'They were North African guys who were really good at maths and science.'

The beginning of every cricket game became a history class. And the war cries weren't nearly as good. 'C'mon the Saracens!' didn't spark the same fire in the belly that a cry of 'Let's Go Taliban!' did. We had to drop the mock firing of our Kalashnikovs. The new name just didn't stick.

During the third game of the tournament, just when we looked to be on the verge of another loss and possible elimination after a dramatic turn in our fortunes, Shahan instinctively began to cry out 'Go Taliban!' It coincided with the week the Americans invaded Afghanistan. But there was no association in our minds. Shahan's call galvanised us as a group and we started firing mock rifles in the air again. Faisal flung himself in to a successful diving catch soon afterwards, before going off the field with a bad back. I bowled an inswinging yorker to take out the batsman's stumps and Shahan threw the wickets down from twenty metres away to create an unlikely run out.

Together we hurtled towards an unexpected victory, a kind of last stand before the flames of our youthful passions flickered away.

8
Work and Women

Tania was dressed for work at the local gourmet grocery
store. She wore dark pants and a white T-shirt, and when
she arrived at the shop she'd don an apron with 'Martelli's'
emblazoned on it in black calligraphic writing. It was her
first part-time job and she was swelling with pride. She
was seventeen and about to sit for her final examinations
at Cheltenham Girls High School. For several years she'd
travelled to school by train but by now we had moved to a
big new house in Epping, which was closer.

'I need something to distract myself. I'm sick of studying,' she told my mother, who worried that a job would
stop her from applying herself but relented, trusting her
daughter's instincts.

Tania had already done a couple of shifts, attending
the cash register or arranging the fruit and vegetables into
neat rows before spraying them with water. Martelli's had a
reputation for stocking produce that was much fresher than
the large supermarket chains like Franklins and Coles. My
mother visited religiously, supplementing her own produce
from the closely nurtured garden in our backyard. Once she

tried to get Tania to sneak some yellow coloured chillis into her shopping bag for free.

I encouraged Tania's interest in work and didn't think it was of any consequence. I reminded my parents that when I was in my final year of high school I'd played a great deal of sport during my exams and had studied more efficiently when I was home because of it. I'd also had part-time jobs but was never very good at keeping them. I lasted a few weeks as a pizza delivery boy and just over a month working on the check-out at Franklins. At the time my parents had no concerns and now I wondered if it was because I was male. Perhaps they thought my Y chromosome protected me from harm or exploitation from other males.

Even though Tania had mentioned the job to our father casually, he didn't seem to be aware of it. That afternoon, when she was on her way out, he arrived home from work. When he asked where she was going, Tania filled him in, and suddenly, something snapped.

He blocked her path to the front door. 'You will not go to work,' he said angrily.

Tania, irritated, tried to walk past him, thinking it was all huff and puff. But my father remained insistent.

'No!' he shouted. 'You will not go to work.'

'Abba, please,' Tania said, confused at the disproportionate response.

'Babur Abba,' my mother chimed in, pleading. 'Please, don't do this. Let her go.'

But Abba wouldn't budge and suddenly a normal afternoon at home descended into a fracas of pushing and

My mother inspecting her new baby,
pleased there was no kidnapping.

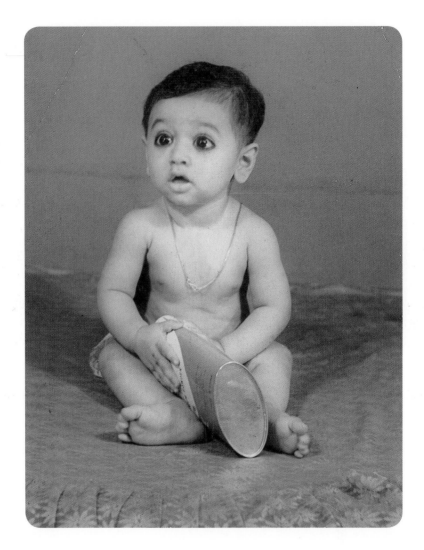

My first photo shoot as a baby. Check out the eyeliner.

Me (*left*) with Rojon and his older brother. We could have been a toddler boy band.

My parents looking fresh-faced, soon after arriving in Australia.

Getting in early with my birthday cake at our first flat in Harris Park.

Above Me sitting with the old man in his photochromatic glasses, on charity-gifted furniture. I suspect the haircut was my father's handiwork.

Top left Tania in her usual Just Peachy outfit, being soothed by my father.

Below left I am still fuming with jealousy after the arrival of Tania.

Above Tania looks less than impressed as her big brother attempts to look caring.

Top left My first days at an Australian school. I suspect I was busting for the toilet after drinking copious amounts of water.

Below left Me with Ramazan, and an intimidatingly tall girl, in our first year of school.

Above Dressed for Victorian England – or perhaps as Bangladeshi extras in a Jane Austen flick.

Opposite above My first day of high school, dressed in oversized clothing bought to extend the life of my expensive uniform. I'm weighed down by a bag full of books and the fear of walking to Toongabbie station in a shirt and tie.

Opposite below Daniel and me in our final year at Grammar. We were a poor man's Jazzy Jeff and the Fresh Prince.

Our group of medical students at Alice before venturing out into remote Aboriginal communities.

The all-conquering team with the unfortunate name.

Above My sister, Tania, preparing to rub turmeric over me and Alina, part of a pre-wedding purification ritual. My headgear is about to fall off.

Top right Alina and me with my paternal grandparents after arriving in my mother's village for post-wedding celebrations.

Below right Is that a Ukrainian Princess Di, spreading joy to the masses of Bangladesh?

Neeever agaaain!

At home with Alina, Katarina and Saskia.

shouting. I held my father back as Tania pushed her way past, weeping as she left the house.

Abba stormed around the house, avoiding any eye contact, picking at tools in the garage and shouting. 'You brainwashed the children,' he called out to my mother, before making a reference to his pride, using the word meaning honour. 'It is not my fault. Shommaan.'

There'd been clues to his growing resentment in the previous months. When my sister attended her high school formal in a long black dress and left in a hired limousine, he'd walked around the house all night growling that he was losing control of the household.

He'd also raised concerns about my plans to take a year off from university in order to travel. He had lamented with family friends that he knew nothing of it and decisions by his children were made with input from their mother only. It coincided with a time when adolescent children in the Bangladeshi community were beginning to expose rifts and conflicts within households. There were instances of parents not attending their children's weddings because of white non-Muslim partners, fathers following their daughters to late night parties and police being called to domestic violence incidents.

I had imagined such stories were reserved for the world of hyper-masculine Arab men but was now watching it unfold within the Bangladeshi community as the Old World ways of family, clan and tradition were inexorably pulled apart. Migrating was fine for educating the children, for becoming wealthy and sending money back home to relatives, but women and children doing their own thing was just not part of the deal. My mother had worked all her life, something that gave us a degree of freedom as we grew up. She gave us pocket money so we could see movies, and go out with friends, activities that seemed superfluous to an academic education in my father's eyes. His own hard upbringing in Bangladesh had built within him a perpetual sense of insecurity, a feeling that everything could disappear in an instant, either through natural disaster, war or higher interest rates. His children roaming free symbolised a failure on his part to uphold a culture and tradition. It was a kind of defeat to the lures of the West.

Abba confessed to feeling downgraded in his role as a father. He felt helpless while he watched his daughter exert her independence and begin to stay out late at night, and worried that his son was becoming too Australianised – drinking alcohol and having girlfriends. After his out-of-character confrontation with Tania, I watched him with his head bowed in the garage, slumped over a plank of wood, clumsily pounding a nail with a hammer. I felt torn. I was angry for his backward behaviour toward Tania and my big brother protective reflex had been sharpened. But I also felt sorry for his sense of loss, his inability to make sense of the world around him. Just as Tania and I had difficulty understanding him, we were like foreigners to him, too.

My father had a reputation in the Bangladeshi community as a quiet, technical man who was something of a 'Mr Fix-it'. He was always invited to family friends' houses to repair washing machines with damaged spin cycles or to seal leaks in car engines. 'Afsar Bhai' – Brother Afsar – was how he became known. He tried to involve me in his excursions, but I failed to gain an interest and lacked any aptitude as a handyman, a deficit that is exposed today in wonky furniture installations or unevenly trimmed lawns.

His anger was uncommon, but sudden and intimidating. I once saw him spontaneously abuse a referee at a Parramatta football game after an unpopular decision, standing suddenly among a rowdy, inebriated crowd to point directly to the uniformed referee to denounce him as a 'bus-tard', shouting in a thick Indian-souding accent. He was met with shouts of approval and support from the onlookers around us. After my initial shock at his outburst, it made me proud.

It was only a year or so before he blew up at Tania that I'd begun to understand him better. During another visit to Bangladesh during the school holidays I watched him relax with family and friends. He smiled and laughed, dressed in a white singlet and striped green lungi, much like the memories I had of him when I was a very young child.

He helped his brothers fling nets into the village pond to catch fish and sat with old school friends in tea shops made from bamboo and thatched roofs. There, he would hold court while relatives and townsfolk spoke to him of their problems, hoping for access to his funds. I learnt from some of his university friends that he had once been a great athlete and had a good sense of humour, sides of him I had never seen growing up.

I understood that there was always a part of him that

was thinking of his family in Bangladesh and ways to help them from our privileged position in Australia. Tania and I joked about the 'Bijoy moments', times when our Australian existence was infiltrated by beliefs inherited from Bangladesh and his village, Bijoyrampur.

When I was about ten, our household was woken by a midnight phone call. I was roused further by the sound of my mother shouting into the receiver, 'Ki?', which means 'What?' in Bengali. Then she called out for my father. I had already learnt that late night phone calls usually related to very sick relatives whose welfare depended upon the speedy transfer of money from my father. Calls were made from small shops in nearby village markets. The lines were invariably unreliable, punctuated by hisses and crackles, and conversations usually began with repeated shouts of 'Hello, hello!' There was a frenetic drama about each morsel of communication.

It was even more serious this time. My grandfather had died after falling off what was known as a van, essentially a flat wooden board positioned on the back of a bicycle which could sit seat between three and four people. He'd landed on his head and suffered a brain haemorrhage and was pronounced dead on arrival at a local hospital. I had almost no relationship with my paternal grandfather. I barely knew what it was like to have grandparents at all, and had little understanding of the way friends felt about their 'Nan' or 'Pop'. I remembered him as a bearded man who prayed five times a day. My mother said he was a simple, loving man who enjoyed good food. He practised homeopathy in the village, distributing tiny pellets of medicine. I tried them several times and enjoyed the sweet taste, but I struggled to feel any affection for the man himself when I was told of his death. I only cared about what it might mean for my father.

I woke in the morning to see my father being consoled by my mother, showing a vulnerability that I had never seen before. He looked pale and his eyes were red from crying and baggy from lack of sleep. Even though it was early, he was on the phone speaking to relatives about the organisation of the rapidly approaching funeral. He was getting angry and yelling into the mouthpiece about why a certain task had not been completed. According to Islamic tradition the burial had to take place within twenty-four hours and it was too soon for my father to fly back for the ceremony.

The contrast with my mother's family could not have been more stark. When we visited Bangladesh her three sisters and younger brothers were animated with emotion, our trips full of singing and physical affection. When the electricity failed, as it often did, the entire family sat in one of the tin bedrooms of the village home and took turns singing to each other or telling a story. Eventually they would turn to Tania and me and ask us to sing a song in English. I had little to offer and often resorted to nursery rhymes. Once, I sang the jingle for a cooking sauce, Chicken Tonight, while I flapped my elbows up and down. I said it was a well known song in Australia.

When Tania returned from her six-hour shift at Martelli's she looked tired and haggard and had tomato stains on her top. She ran upstairs and went straight to her room. My father tried to make amends, walking in sheepishly soon afterwards and appealing to her affectionately. 'Ma – I am sorry,' he said.

'Go away,' Tania responded.

My father listened and did as she asked, closing the door gently. For the next few days after the incident he remained quiet and continued to offer olive branches to Tania – lifts to the train station, cups of tea and unfettered access to the telephone. The tension settled eventually.

My father tried to make amends by expanding his house-work contributions and taking a greater interest in Tania's activities. He admitted to my mother that he was only able to show love for his children through anger. Having seen his family's emotionally muted interactions in the village, I understood what he meant, and felt sorry for him all over again.

Months later, he started giving advice to other parents. 'You should listen to what your children want,' he told a family friend, suddenly becoming an advocate for the democratisation of Bangladeshi families.

Tania continued to work and stayed out late on rare occasions. My father continued to grapple with the modifi-cation of his sense of masculinity. In the end, he decided to go fishing more often, but was unable to attract my interest and company. His weekend-long forays to the Hawkesbury River were usually a solitary affair.

9
Illegal Alien

The border official shoved me into a room and slammed the door shut. I was alone. I sat on a wooden stool with shaky foundations. The room was bare with nothing but a big poster of Mahathir Mohamad on one wall. It felt like some kind of torture strategy, to severely limit any stimulation until I descended into madness. I was seething with anger, and began to shout out, threatening my captors with the wrath of the Australian High Commission.

'They'll suspend all aid to your stupid country after this gets out in the news!' I yelled, not at all conscious of my melodramatic tone. 'I'm Australian, you idiots!'

I started thinking the worst, that I might be thrown into a jail like the Bangkok Hilton and gang raped by menacing Malay tax evaders before I slowly withered into a skeletal fraction of my former self. I thought of my family, my mother tilling her luscious vegetable garden, my father fixing household appliances and my sister on the phone talking late into the night to her friends. Abba would say that he had told me so, that I should never have given up my studies to wander off for a year of aimless travel.

After three years at university I felt bored and realised that the concept of body mechanics didn't get my intellectual juices flowing. Despite finding something wondrous in the matrix pattern of blood vessels under a microscope or seeing up close the extraordinary precision of a beating heart, for some reason I wasn't entirely inspired by my studies. It was a long way from my fantasy of university as a place brimming with challenging ideas and experiences. I was only twenty-one years old. In reality, I was just one of a large percentage of medical students who fell into the course because they scored high marks in their Higher School Certificates and were lured by the idea of being a doctor, egged on by the drama of hospital soaps that seemed to dominate television at the time. This was particularly true given I was from an Asian background. It wasn't that my parents pushed me into it, but there was still a subtle cultural meme that being a doctor was the pinnacle of professional achievement. I was exactly the kind of person the new postgraduate courses, which aimed to attract people with a passion and commitment to Medicine as a vocation, were trying to get rid of.

So, afflicted as I was with a kind of middle-class affluenza, the same kind of existential malaise that I'd criticised the children of wealthy families of complaining about, I postponed studying at one of the nation's most prestigious institutions for an education in the school of hard knocks. Or rather, my plan was to take a year off to travel around the world, something of an Australian rite of passage. My decision sent an emotional shockwave through my parents, who worried that I was leaving my studies to become a hobo. Within days of the news reaching the Bangladeshi community there were rumours that I had become addicted to drugs and had failed my course.

'He had such potential. I'm so sorry,' said a friend of my father's, patting him on the shoulder in sympathy when he was informed of my plans at a dinner party.

In order to fund my trip I worked for several months doing data entry for a pathology company. I typed up patient details and filled in forms. I became something of a star recruit because I could interpret the scrawled handwriting of doctors and was able translate the obscure medical terminology written on some of the forms. Phaeochromocytoma? That's a tumour of the adrenal gland. Tachycardia? Just a fast heart rate. And otitis media? Well, that's a fancy term for a middle-ear infection. Those years at university – all the rote learning for examinations and miming songs for university revues – were paying off at last.

Europe was to be the first leg of my trip and Spain was my first port of call. There, while briefly studying Spanish, I met Marcus, a long-haired Belgian historian. He gave me mind-altering drugs and quoted from Nietsche. 'God is dead, Tanveer,' he said one night at a bar, before passing me a book. I'd never heard of the philosopher before and suddenly felt a sense of purpose, albeit about the ideas of someone who theorised that perhaps man had no purpose.

I travelled for months all over Europe, from Italy to Germany, Greece and Sweden, and after spending many hours alone, reading, observing and thinking, I became more and more introspective. After living all my life at home with a loving mother who did everything for me, I was literally forced into greater independence. Arriving late one night in Florence I discovered there was no accommodation to be found so I slept overnight with three homeless men at the main train station. One had chunks of bread in his bushy grey beard, another had rosy red cheeks and offered me a swig of his Chianti and the third, wearing a red and black AC Milan football shirt, shared his woollen blanket with me. We settled down for the night next to the ticketing counter, the maroon carriages of an empty train on Platform Uno our silent guardian. Resigned to my fate I practised my amateur Italian.

'Per favore, non rubare le mie cose,' I said hesitantly, asking my companions not to rob me.

I needn't have bothered. They felt sorry for me in my cheap clothes and single backpack. The following morning, when I went looking for a youth hostel, one of them suggested I visit them again if I had any problems.

As I travelled on, I was surprised to hear the familiar lilt of Bengali. It was usually spoken by young men carrying wooden boxes filled with beads, souvenirs and postcards, the vendors who set up on the corners of most European plazas. I approached one of them on a bus in Rome after visiting the Colosseum. His name was Jamil and he introduced me to his brother, Malik. They both wore white T-shirts with 'I love Paris' in bright pink, although they'd never been to the famous city.

Excited to meet a fellow native speaker, they tried to

give me their products for free – magnets of the Vatican, a miniature Pantheon and an 'Italians do it better' T-shirt.

'Please, bhai. You come and stay with us,' Jamil said, offering me Bangladeshi sweets as inducement. He lived in a poor suburb half an hour away. The roads were in need of repair and many of the shops seemed unattended or up for lease, their grates locked with padlocks. Scooters and cars whizzed up the main street and old men sat on folding chairs on the footpath.

The apartment was tiny but had very high ceilings and enormous shuttered windows. There were eight of us crowded into two bedrooms, including two Somalis. It was like a hostel for illegal immigrants from some of the poorest countries in the world. I enjoyed feeling like I was one of them, on the fringes of society in the ill-defined landscape of unbelonging, although I was exposed as a fraud later that night when Jamil noticed my Euro-Rail pass and American Express credit card lying on the bunk bed.

They had all arrived in Italy illegally after travelling across Asia or the Mediterranean. Jamil had flown to Pakistan and hitched a ride in a truck across the Middle East before getting a boat from Turkey to the Italian port of Brindisi. For hours they questioned me about how my parents had managed to migrate to Australia and whether I might be able to help them gain access there.

'Tanveer bhai, Australia is good place to live, yes?' Malik said. 'I would love to have a kangaroo as a pet.'

I woke in the morning to watch them thread beads on leather necklaces and make puppets out of balloons. They ate rice with chilli and boiled egg for breakfast, sharing it collegially. Malik showed me a letter that he was writing to his mother. It was full of lies to lift her spirits: he was working in an office job and would soon have enough money to come home and marry someone of her choosing.

After six months of travel I grew weary of the predictability of the backpacking trail with its well-trod tourist landmarks and often approached men selling souvenirs, asking them where they were from. Whether they were from Bangladesh, Pakistan or Morocco they had similar stories of epic journeys only to arrive in the West as illegal immigrants to undertake lowly jobs. But it still seemed preferable compared to the lack of opportunity in their homelands.

The experience reminded me of the two house guests who stayed with us in Toongabbie when I was a child, perhaps seven or eight years old. Shagor and Hafeez lived with us for several weeks, one sleeping on a fold-out sofa in our lounge room and the other on our orange floral couch near the kitchen. They worked for cash as dishwashers in small restaurants and told us about how they had to evade immigration officers knocking at their door.

Shagor was fair-skinned and usually dressed in a business shirt and trousers. My mother told me he was from a wealthy family in Sylhet, the tea growing region in Bangladesh. Hafeez sported a curly black moustache that turned up playfully at the ends and had a thin scar across his cheek. He had a wife back in Bangladesh and carried a photo of her in his wallet: a young woman dressed in a bright yellow sari. Her long black hair flowed down to her waist and she held a lit candle in an upturned palm. Hafeez hoped to bring her to Australia one day.

At night, I overheard them talking quietly with my parents about their circumstances. My mother kept making remarks of sympathy. 'Oh ma go,' she said anxiously. 'Ki hobe?' Or 'Oh my God' and 'What will happen?' For those few weeks, a continuous supply of sweets came from Amma in the kitchen, from rice pudding to doughy balls covered in syrup.

Shagor and Hafeez wanted to stay in Australia but had no obvious way of achieving residency. I kept hearing them mention the term PR, which I later found out meant Permanent Residency. Apparently my family had it and it meant we could stay as long as we wanted. I made the association with a ceremony that occurred at Parramatta Town Hall, an event where an official welcomed us as new Australians, an Aboriginal man with white face paint played didgeridoo and my parents hummed the national anthem because they didn't know the words.

'They are illegal,' my father explained when I asked about their situations.

I was a little shocked. They seemed like nice people yet they were apparently like criminals. We were legal because my father, like our family friends, arrived with qualifications in computing, accountancy or medicine. People like Shagor and Hafeez came as either tourists or students and simply did what they could to stay. The Bangladeshi community helped them when they could, but did so at arm's length for fear of getting into trouble themselves.

I must have been almost fifteen when my mother announced one afternoon that Shagor and Hafeez were planning to drop in for a visit. We hadn't seen them for years.

'I think they have got their PR,' she told me.

Hours later they arrived, cruising triumphantly into our driveway in a blue Toyota Corolla sedan. I rushed out with my mother onto our tiny tiled porch, ready to welcome them like diplomats greeting a plane on the tarmac. My father was pruning the roses in the front yard and waved to our guests with his thick gardening gloves.

Stepping out of the Corolla with them were two women, both dressed in saris. One looked Asian in appearance and walked awkwardly in her heels as she held the shawl of her sari in one hand. Shagor smiled broadly as he held a bag of wrapped presents. Hafeez had shaved his moustache and had a modern haircut.

A feast followed and we learnt that Shagor and Hafeez had indeed achieved their dream of permanent residency and had since married – Shagor returning to Bangladesh and marrying the daughter of a wealthy merchant from his home region of Sylhet, and Hafeez marrying a Filipino woman he met in Sydney, a nursing assistant in an aged care home.

My mother later told me that Shagor had paid a fee of thousands of dollars to an older woman in her forties who lived in country New South Wales. They were married for a year but later separated and divorced, as was the agreement.

His prize was to be finally – and formally – accepted as an Australian. Hafeez hadn't been able to return to see his wife since there was a risk of never being able to come back. She'd grown impatient and remarried. After much sadness and despair, he eventually met the Filipino girl who was already an Australian citizen.

As I travelled the world, it became clear that there was a parallel world of Bangladeshis who lived like our ex house guests, working odd jobs as taxi drivers and kitchen hands and keeping one ear out for potential run-ins with immigration officers, a kind of international cat and mouse. My travels graduated to become an exploration of expatriate Bangladeshi migrants. I was riveted by their marked differences compared to my own experiences of relative wealth, comfort and social mobility in Australia.

When I was returning to Sydney via Malaysia, I visited Titu, my mother's cousin, who was working in a fax machine factory in Johor Bahru. Titu grew up in the house next to my mother's in Dihi. His father was the younger brother of my grandfather and known for being a playful larrikin. He used to take my mother and her sister, Bulu, to watch Bollywood films in the city but told my grandfather they were buying textbooks. He later became very religious after losing a child to cholera. Titu was one of his younger sons and known for being slightly odd as a child, often screaming and shouting even as a teenager. His face was unusually thin and looked squashed in from both sides, as if his head had run out of space in the womb.

Titu's job was to check each machine after the plastic panels and metal bits were all put together by his colleagues, each one having a specific task of either placing in a screw, fitting together different panels or packing the finished product. The completed machines were all exported to Japan.

I spent two days with him and stayed with his workmates in a free bunk bed in their quarters. Much like my experience in Italy, Titu slept each night with thirty others, all pressed up against each other in bunks barely a metre apart. They shared a single bathroom with a rusty shower and the kind of toilet where you squatted over a hole. Relieving myself reminded me of the ear-squat punishment and I grabbed my ears for old time's sake.

In the mornings the men had to wait to use the facilities, lining up in a long queue. They didn't seem to mind. Their attitude seemed a universal one of grinning and bearing it, along with their three-dollar-a-day wages, twelve-hour days and six-day working weeks. It was Dickensian, a reminder that the rank and file of the world economy had not disappeared, they had merely shifted.

Titu had been there for almost two years. I had met him several times during my visits to Bangladesh. He was only a few years older than me and would always call me 'Mama', which means maternal uncle. Despite not being much of a student, barely getting through high school and not having any work experience other than tilling the family farm, Titu had been resourceful enough to gain access to the guest worker program. His family had to pay for the privilege, the fee sucked up by a human resources company that supplied the cheapest labour in the world for countries like Malaysia, Singapore and Saudi Arabia.

Once they arrived, workers were used to perform the most menial jobs for pitiful amounts of money. But this kind of work was considered prestigious to poor farmers and unskilled workers in the city. They could say they worked in the 'bidesh', the Bengali word for overseas, which has glamorous connotations of wealth and freedom, even if they were cleaning toilets in Dubai.

Titu had already sent money back to his family, buying them a new television and a stereo system and helping to send his youngest sister, Sushila, to university. Along with my mother, he was one of a tiny handful of people from the area who had been overseas. His family enjoyed the gifts, especially since they'd seen the same gleaming Western products fill the household of their neighbours, my grandparents.

Titu taught me some Malay words: 'Aba kaba?' – 'How are you?' – and 'Anda kantik', meaning 'You are beautiful'. I suspected he might have some kind of love interest and he later introduced me to a Filipino girl, a shy young woman in pigtails called Alice. I imagined my uncle's relationship with Alice as an apt romantic and political union, given the primary export for both countries was the cheap labour of its people.

One night, while we ate the boiled rice and dahl he had cooked for us, Titu held back tears while he told me that he and Alice had considered a romance but found it very difficult to manage in the crowded quarters of their living arrangements and long working hours. 'We never had a chance, Mama,' he said, shaking his head with his eyes downcast.

They'd once hired a hotel room near the Singapore border, but Alice decided her Christian faith could not allow for sex before marriage. Besides, Alice had told him that she could never convert to Islam, something Titu said would be essential if his parents were ever to accept her. I was already experienced with the issue of God infiltrating relationships, not to mention the bedroom, and patted him sympathetically on the shoulder.

As for the men, there were separate lodging arrangements for the women, which included groups from Indonesia, Bangladesh and the Phillipines. Titu and several of his colleagues lamented that the Bangladeshi girls weren't interested in them because they thought they were cheap. I remembered my mother had made the same complaint about my father a few times. The women preferred Malaysian–Tamil men who treated them lavishly, buying them gifts and jewellery.

Titu shook his head and waved his arms in frustration. 'The ladies don't understand that we have responsibilities to our families, eh, bhai,' he said, looking at me as if I could sympathise.

To cheer him up, I told him about some of my own romantic failures during my travels: the German academic who emoted about her great connection with me before introducing me to her Spanish bullfighter boyfriend; the Welsh aspiring podiatrist who said that in spite of my apparent intelligence, she felt all Australians were crass and primitive; and an Israeli girl I met on a Greek island who told me she loved dark men before letting me know that she felt the Israeli–Palestinian conflict forbade her from being with a Muslim.

The day I left Titu, my plan was to get a bus over the border into Singapore so that I could catch a plane back to Sydney. After a year of travelling I was finally ready to go home and start the next phase of my life. At the Malaysia–Singapore border, the bus pulled over, allowing the passengers to be assessed and processed by the immigration officials. It was a routine procedure. I joined a queue with my fellow travellers from the bus who were mostly Chinese–Singaporean tourists, a small number of darker skinned men with simpler clothing who were likely to be Malay and a handful of white tourists.

When it was my turn, I approached the glass window of the processing office. I smiled at the young official in his blue uniform and handed him my passport.

As he flicked through the pages he looked immediately curious, surveying the various stamps I'd collected from my travels around the world. He nodded and seemed impressed when he saw the seals from each of the European countries I'd visited and the bald eagle from America, where I'd stayed with a friend in his college dorm in Boston. Then his eyes started shifting back and forth from the pages to my face. Finally he flicked to the front page where there was a sober photo of me which had been taken several years before. It had grown tattered and there were stains on the edge of the page. All of a sudden he stiffened, focusing on a particular detail.

Flustered, he said something in Malay while pointing at my passport.

'I only speak English,' I said, shaking my head.

He showed me the entry on my passport where it said 'Country of Birth'. Mine had Bangladesh next to it. I nodded. 'That's where I was born,' I said, hoping he understood.

He continued to shake his head and asked for advice from a colleague. 'Alla mak.'

An older, moustachioed guard wearing a white prayer hat looked at my passport and shrugged his shoulders. But the young official remained perturbed and waved the other passengers behind me on to another booth. 'Cepat!' he shouted, waving them away.

I was getting impatient. I explained that I had been visiting my uncle who worked in a factory and that I was now travelling to Singapore so I could return to Australia. He ignored me, then directed me inside the office where he eyed me suspiciously and asked me in broken English how I got an Australian passport. When I realised what was going on, it was the trigger for my anger and outrage.

'I am an Australian citizen!' I shouted, staring him down. 'You might notice that my English is better than yours!'

And that's when I was hauled into the bare room with only a poster of Malaysia's benevolent despot to keep me company. My teeth were clenched and my limbs stiffened, like I was ready for combat. I knew that making a scene might get me in more trouble so I tried to talk myself down. The indignity of it all was that, in the border official's eyes, I was a lowly Bangladeshi who, like my uncle, could only be a foreign worker.

After a few minutes, during which I imagined myself as the next Mandela or Gandhi fighting against the discrimination of the poor and oppressed, a distinguished looking middle-aged Chinese man in a brown suit walked in. He was carrying my passport.

'I'm very sorry sir,' he said in a clipped tone. 'It was a mistake by one of our new workers. There has been a real problem with fake passports recently.' Then he handed me my passport. 'Please accept our apologies.'

I grabbed my passport, which then felt like a lifeline, a badge of my superior citizenship. 'I'm going to let the Australian embassy know of your incompetence,' I said, suddenly full of my own importance. Somehow I had inherited some of the bias of the border official.

But honestly. Hadn't he noticed that I was dressed in sandals, a ripped T-shirt and carried an oversized back-pack? Only wealthy Westerners would subject themselves to such limitless freedom.

10
Shooting with Bill

'You don't have any blackfella in you, do you, doc?' said my first patient for the night.

'Kinda. I'm from India, or thereabouts,' I said while walking him into the single room of the clinic. The grey walls were covered with promotional posters, everything from what to do for snake bite to protection from sexually transmitted disease. Marilyn, the Aboriginal health worker, applied pressure to the bandage she was holding to Bill's head.

He was covered in blood. Thick clumps of his black hair were plastered down in red coagulating pools of the stuff. The blood was thickest at the back of his head where a deep wound was visible, triangular with sharp edges.

'What happened, Sir?' I asked, attempting to sound confident despite the fact I was still only a medical student.

'I got a headache,' he said with little emotion, as if his tax return might be due. 'Me wife whacked me head with them axe.'

It was payday. Bill smelled of alcohol and still held a can of VB in his right hand. His skin was heavily wrinkled and he looked to be in about his mid fifties. Wearing a torn, sleeveless football jersey and white shorts that drooped down to his rickety knees, Bill looked at me furtively then turned away, seeking reassurance from Marilyn.

'We'll have to stitch it up. I'm a training doctor up from Sydney,' I said.

Bill seemed to relax, made eye contact and then began to grimace, as if I had given him permission to reveal his pain.

It was late in the evening, about ten o'clock, and I'd just stepped out of my one-bedroom townhouse opposite the clinic. My optimistic attempt to sneak a few hours of sleep before midnight was foiled. In a few hours the inevitable stream of patients with injuries after payday drinks would begin to filter in – falls, assaults and dizzy patients whose blood sugar levels had fallen too low.

Other than the clinic, the town of Elliott had a pub, a milk bar, a police station, a school and a sandy, rocky golf course where the greens were called browns. The whole place was no bigger than one square kilometre. The locals gathered along metal benches and wooden tables arranged around two basketball courts. A cobbled path led to the clinic, barely a hundred metres away. Many sat down with their sixpacks of beer and cigarettes on the court.

The younger boys wore T-shirts with American team logos like the Chicago Bulls and the Los Angeles Lakers. I could see one kid, a teenager I had treated earlier that day for a respiratory infection, attempt to take beer away from his already drunk mother, only to be scolded and waved away. The boy's shoulders sagged and he walked back to a group of his friends who all seemed to be keeping watch on their own parents as they played with a basketball in one corner.

I'd arrived the day before, part of a new program set up for medical students to work in remote Aboriginal communities in the Northern Territory. It was my final year of university before graduating, the finishing line of a gruelling six years of study.

I was more focussed on my studies after a year of travelling and had completed my fourth and fifth years without much of a hitch. I had also started writing for the university newspaper, *Honi Soit*, finding an outlet for my new passion for politics, literature and history, awoken by my experiences overseas. I wrote an article about the pharmaceutical sponsorship of university parties that annoyed a student politician, who searched me out to educate me about my misconceptions about the funding of student organisations. I felt a thrill that my words had the power to piss people off.

I had also regained my interest in general medicine after completing a compulsory stint overseas the year before, where I treated patients with cholera and diptheria in an international hospital in Bangladesh. There were rows and rows of people dying from illnesses that had been eradicated in rich countries like Australia and it was my job to keep them hydrated with saline. I became a casualty myself after contracting a rare form of liver disease – Hepatitis E. My skin was pale yellow for over a month and I lost ten kilos. I looked like an oversized canary.

When I returned home, one of my lecturers, who was a world expert in infections, was very excited to run tests on me, given my illness was recorded in only three countries at the time: Bangladesh, Bolivia and Chile. It all felt like an elaborate trick by mighty powers from above to make me more committed to medicine, like a hackneyed movie plot where the emotionally distant burnt-out doctor is forced to confront his cynicism by contracting cancer or some other life-threatening illness.

It was good preparation for the Northern Territory and I arrived in Elliott to treat the local Aborigines with a spirit of excitement and idealism. I had already been warned by a physician at a short two-day orientation program in Alice Springs that the town was rough and I would see plenty of action. He made it sound like I was going to Afghanistan or Iraq. After his lecture I walked up the main street of Alice Springs and noticed that there was a high proportion of Aboriginal men walking around with bandages on a limb or around their head. I remember thinking that if Alice was the quieter town then I was in a lot of trouble.

I spent almost an hour stitching up Bill's wounds. When I gave him a tetanus injection I noticed a fiery red swelling on his arm that looked infected and started him on antibiotics as well. Marilyn sat with me throughout it all and helped relax Bill through the pain of the procedures. When I was finished, she pulled out his file from a metal cabinet in the corner of the room, next to a poster about genital warts. Benjamin William Foster was his full name and he was thirty-seven years old.

Now that his pain had settled, Bill began to talk more freely. I knew that eye contact could be intimidating and rude but I felt a little ridiculous looking at either Marilyn or the filing cabinet while we talked about his injury.

'Me wife did it for them payback,' he told me after some gentle urging from Marilyn. I knew that payback was a common way of settling scores for some of the more traditional Aboriginal men, especially among the older generation. I never imagined that it could happen between husband and wife.

When I asked him to explain, Bill stopped talking and started wincing in pain again.

'Bill cheated on his wife with her cousin in Tennant Creek, the one who plucks her eyebrows, didn't you, Bill?' Marilyn interjected.

Bill dropped his head in shame. I felt my eyes widen and my mouth gape open. It felt as if I was playing a walk-on role in a *Days of our Lives* episode, only with a cast of Aboriginal actors.

I quickly reverted to a more non-judgemental doctor pose. 'I'm just interested in your health, Bill,' I reassured him.

Sober now after an hour in the medical clinic, Bill walked out with a bandage taped across the back of his head and a cheery demeanour. 'I'm gunna take you hunting them bush turkey, doc. What do you reckon?' he said.

I nodded but was distracted by the growing line of patients. On that first night, Marilyn and I treated almost thirty people, mostly related to falls or fights. I had to transfer one man to the larger hospital in Tennant Creek for emergency surgery, the ambulance driving two hundred kilometres to come and pick him up. It was the most work I'd ever done as a medical student.

The clinic was run by a nurse who was originally from South Africa. Lesley was smoking a cigarette outside the front door when I turned up the next day. Her conversation was so full of words like strewth and bloody hell that it felt like she'd just completed a course in dinky-di Australianisms. She'd been working in Elliott for a year, starting afresh after a failed marriage. In the few days I'd spent in Alice Springs I'd already noticed that many people who lived in the Northern Territory were fleeing something – tattered relationships, failed careers or society in general – or at least, that's the way it seemed to me. I could certainly see the appeal of escaping your past and starting anew amid the sacred natural beauty of ancient rocks and national parks.

Outside the clinic, traces of the night before had largely disappeared, apart from the many empty cans of beer. There were only two teenagers practising basketball shots on the court from the foul line. It could have been the night after a college party at university.

Marilyn was already inside wearing a blue uniform, a collared shirt and long skirt, with a thin grey stethoscope hanging around her neck. She was taking sugar and blood pressure readings from a group of patients attending a diabetes clinic. She'd grown up in Darwin. Her father was an American Mormon pastor who married and later divorced her mother, an Aboriginal woman. 'I went to go see Duran

Duran in LA ,' she told me when we met for the first time. 'I want to have Simon Le Bon's baby.'

Marilyn identified strongly with the community at Elliott. She was also aware of her privileged status. Health workers have great prestige as the cultural conduit between doctors, nurses and the rest of the Aboriginal community.

Later that day I ran into Bill at the petrol station, which was attached to the pub. Some of the locals joked that it was convenient to get drunk and then sniff petrol, a comment used as a kind of stereotype meter to test new arrivals.

Bill was in a white Land Cruiser with three other Aboriginal men. He pointed to his bandage as he wound down the window.

'Ay,' he said to his companions, no longer slurring his speech but wearing the same bloodstained clothes from the night before, 'this is the new doc.'

'Hi there, fellas,' I said, lifting my hand in greeting.

The others nodded and grunted. One of them was trying to light a cigarette in the back seat.

'Are you going walkabout?' I joked.

'It's sorta like that. We're drivin to Coles,' Bill answered. 'I'll come and find you tomorrow, doc.'

They sped off down the Stuart Highway. The nearest supermarket was a hundred kilometres away.

Out there in the middle of Australia I had never felt more like a city slicker. The locals walked and talked slowly. There was nothing to do. While there was a beauty in the vast emptiness of the landscape, I missed the noise and activity of Sydney. Every ten minutes or so a car would pass through the town, usually a ute or a four-wheel drive travelling at very high speeds. Back then the Territory had no speed limits on its highways.

The population of Elliott was barely a couple of hundred people. While Bangladesh is known for the highest density of people on the planet, in the Northern Territory I was now experiencing the opposite, the least densely populated region in the world.

I went to the pub for lunch, choosing between two minute noodles and a fried pork chop. I placed my order, the pork chop, with the Dutch bartender. Albert was a backpacker with spiky blond hair who wore a singlet with the word Thailand on it and had a fake tattoo of a snake on his shoulder. Like all the Dutch people I have ever met, Albert was tall. 'No veggies until tomorrow,' he told me, adding that I could have chips from the milk bar next door.

As I ate, Albert and I got talking. He had been travelling for almost six months through Asia, New Zealand and now Australia. He'd finished his studies in a small university in Rotterdam and planned to do a masters degree in engineering when he returned after a year of travel. He felt less foreign than most people I'd met in the Territory.

'You know, I like to take photos of the road kill I find – kangaroos, wombats, lizards,' he said after a few drinks. 'I think they would make an amusing coffee table book back in Holland.' He broke into peals of laughter, his head locked in a high frequency nodding movement.

The next morning Bill knocked loudly on my door. Even though he'd told me he was coming, I hadn't really expected it. He was wearing a faded Akubra and a khaki stockman's outfit. He looked clean and energetic, a stark contrast to my Saturday morning lethargy. I didn't have to work; a doctor from Adelaide was covering for the weekend. Bill gave me pituri, native tobacco, to chew so I wouldn't feel tired and motioned for me to follow him.

'Today you gunna come walkabout, doc,' Bill giggled, striding rapidly away from the clinic. He led me to a white fibro house a few hundred metres away, across a bitumen road. The white Land Cruiser was parked out the front and two men, both familiar from the day before, were sitting in the back.

I peeked inside the house. It was neat and plain, and I could see a refrigerator and a tap for running water. Two women were sitting on the back patio. It was a far cry from the corrugated iron housing and lack of basic amenities I had pictured before my arrival.

Bill loaded the car with air rifles, a case of beer and a spare esky, which was for the bush turkeys. One of Bill's companions introduced himself as Bob, Bill's cousin. He was overweight and had long black hair. He shook my hand before returning to his football magazine. Both Bill and Bob worked with the local mechanic. The other man in the back was Charlie.

First we stopped off at the pub to pick up Albert. I'd convinced Bill the Dutch tourist would enjoy the trip, too. As we drove out to what he called his 'special hunting ground' Bill broke into song, singing up his country, the land we were travelling through. He was dingo. This was where dingo had travelled, where dingo still is. He was singing dingo.

Albert and I nodded with sensitivity before Bob broke up and told me that Bill was bullshitting. He barely knew the words of the song. It had been a long time since his late father had taught them to him. Bill, Bob and Charlie were all originally from Katherine, a few hundred kilometres north. They still had lots of family there and would visit most weekends.

We drove for about half an hour, much of it on dirt tracks away from the highway. As we listened to Cold Chisel, Albert and I started drinking the beer but our hosts declined. Bob and Charlie said their livers were shot and they were trying to cut down. Bill said that he hadn't drunk as heavily as he had the other night for a long time.

'I gotta remember to have some dinner before I hit the grog next time,' he said while adjusting the rear vision mirror.

We eventually arrived and were surrounded by bushy scrub that looked no different to anything we had passed for the previous half-hour. This was one of Bill's special hunting zones. The grass was virtually orange and the dirt was blood red.

I carried an air rifle awkwardly, attempting to be quiet. We'd been walking in the scrub for a few hundred metres when we saw the first turkeys. There were two pecking at the ground side by side. Their brown feathers were pretty good camouflage but their blue plumage didn't serve them well at all.

Bill and Bob started shooting right away and, from what I could tell, missed by a mile. I tried, having shot an air rifle once before with my friend Daniel on his family property, before the turkeys scurried deeper in the scrub.

We walked on slowly through the bushes. 'You know, doc, some of my mob can tell a kangaroo is around just by seeing some trees out of place,' said Bill. 'But me, I just wait till I see 'em hopping around.'

Then Bill bent down to inspect something on the ground.

'Are they animal tracks, mate?' I asked expectantly.

'Nah, but I found a two-dollar coin,' he beamed with satisfaction, revealing a gap where his missing front teeth should have been. He held up a jagged rock, before beginning to cackle.

'Don't think we're all doing that Dreamtime and walkabout stuff, doc,' Charlie interrupted, holding his rifle down by his side. 'I never threw a spear in me life.'

Our hunt continued with little success. We sighted several other birds but were too slow or inaccurate to make a kill. 'Sorry doc. I've been 'ere times when we'd 'ave killed a couple of kangaroos and an emu by now,' Bill said. 'Maybe we should do a dance or something for you two.'

Having failed to catch lunch, we bought chicken and chips from the local milk bar on the way home. Albert went back to the pub to start his shift and I followed Bill and his posse back to their place, where we ate our lunch on the back patio. Sitting there I realised that Bill and I had more in common than I first thought. We'd both been cut off from rich cultural and spiritual traditions. I was out of practice with my ancestral language, couldn't read Bengali and barely knew my relatives.

I didn't go hunting again during my two-month stay. I grew lazy and socialised with the other health workers, the dietitians, nurses and medical students. I witnessed many more shocking health problems, from dialysis patients in their thirties, kids going deaf from repeated, untreated ear infections and teenage mums who didn't know they were pregnant until their third trimester, just a couple of months before they gave birth. On one occasion I accompanied a senior doctor on a plane to deliver the baby of a thirteen-year-old mother in the middle of the desert.

I saw Bill when he returned to have his wound checked and several times after that. His head had healed well and his wife had taken him back. He said he was very wary of cheating again. Then he apologised for not finding me some turkey, but brought me chewing tobacco and beer as a gift instead.

'We still got time to make you into a blackfella, doc,' he said.

11
Village Honeymoon

My mother says that white people are like goats and we are like cows. What she means is that nature didn't mean for such different groups to be together. The subject of marriage was always a tough one for me. My parents were desperate for me to marry a girl from Bangladesh, even if it meant returning there to find one over the Christmas holidays. It was to compensate for leaving their family and culture, a way of holding onto the past. On past visits my father wanted to place advertisements in the local newspapers, something along the lines of 'Doctor with Australian Citizenship Seeks Marriage. Fair, Educated Girls Preferred.'

Arranged marriages were common within the community. My friend Ash had one. After being introduced to suitable girls through relatives while in Australia, the plan was to meet the pick of the crop in person months later in Bangladesh. It started on email before progressing to the telephone. Ash claimed it was love at first phone call with his eventual wife, Binni.

He had difficulty explaining to work colleagues how a

two-week holiday transformed him from a bachelor into a married man with a gold wedding ring on his finger. I'd observed others return from holidays newly married, their parents beaming and bragging about the new spouse's high status family. There was a prevailing view that marrying white women was destined to end in divorce, that Westerners didn't have the same sense of commitment to family, children and tradition. Horror stories trickled throughout the community.

'Did you know Raju's wife, Betty, left him for a plumber after just one year of marriage? She couldn't even cook a decent vindaloo,' I once overheard a family friend tell my mother. Amma shook her head sadly. I knew she was worried I might be another Raju.

And she was right.

Alina and I were married in a hybrid ceremony in the gardens of Sydney's Vaucluse House. It was a secular ceremony but included rings and was supplemented with a rice-eating ritual. Our mothers read poetry about nature and romance by Rabindranath Tagore. The wedding was preceded two days before by a henna ceremony, held on Australia Day. The tradition is to rub turmeric on the bodies of the bride and groom as part of a purification ritual, after which both are fed sweets by the guests until their stomachs explode. Alina opted for a watered down version so she could apply tanning cream for the wedding.

My mother had been growing marigolds for six months prior to the event in preparation, hoping to bring to life the colours and spectacle of weddings from the subcontinent.

She watched *Monsoon Wedding* over and over to keep her motivation up. After spending the first week of our honeymoon lazing around the Thai island of Koh Phi Phi, sipping cocktails and eating buffets, Alina and I were on board a flight to Dhaka.

Alina and I had met five years earlier. I was an intern doctor working horrendous hours and doing night shifts. I'd become a regular at the local twenty-four hour pub because of a badly modified body clock. My flatmate, Melissa, was a newly qualified lawyer and was studying with Alina at the College of Law in the city, a short course that rubber stamps graduates for work as professional lawyers. She also knew my Bangladeshi friend Shahan, who had already suggested that we could be good match.

We were introduced at a pizza restaurant in a posh city hotel. Alina had just returned from a trip through Eastern Europe with her mother and sister. With the travel glow of a rejuvenated spirit, she made me laugh with her impression of a Ukrainian accent, the country where her mother was born. They'd visited her mother's extended family's village and her great uncle had asked how many cows they owned in Australia.

I liked that she had an ethnic background. It meant she would have a better insight into the workings of my own family – the obligations, the importance of food and the overhang of tradition. I was attracted to her round face and her obvious intelligence. She made references to Tudor England and the Russian revolution. I had a feeling my mother would like her.

We hit it off immediately and I asked her out days later, egged on by Melissa. She opened up about her parents' divorce and how it had scarred her. When she began to cry, I could see her as a little girl. She began telling her friends that we had lots in common, in particular our star sign – we were both Virgos – and our HSC results.

After living together for a couple of years, first in a share house and then alone, we got engaged. My first attempt at proposing marriage was a failure. I'd carefully packed the ring for our four-year anniversary holiday in Malaysia but in my fits of pre-proposal anxiety I'd forgotten to bring any decent clothes. Alina was fuming.

'You didn't even bring a nice outfit to celebrate our anniversary!' she yelled on the first night, demanding that we had a repeat dinner back home. I returned to the hotel room dejected, the ring still hidden in the pocket of my old trousers.

Two weeks later I proposed with more success. I recited a poem over dinner at a Sydney waterfront restaurant.

Luckily my parents' views about mixed marriage had softened, helped by the fact that they aren't religious and there was no expectation for Alina to convert. She may well have been persuaded to wear a headscarf but only to cover her Celtic skin from burning, a trait inherited from her father's side. There was also a growing number of arranged marriages between Bangladeshis in the community that were ending in divorce, a development that weakened the long held arguments against marrying foreigners.

It took some time, almost the entire time we were

boyfriend and girlfriend, but Amma could see we were in love. She was impressed by Alina's family and her Ukrainian roots. Tania was also a key ally, helping to ease my mother's initial concerns that Alina would be unable to connect with my family. Gaining my mother's approval was a great relief.

Alina's parents were easier to convince. Her father, Peter, is an Englishman who met her mother, Marika, while she was living in London. He loves rugby so much that he wants his ashes spread across Twickenham Stadium. Even though they were divorced they did everything together with their daughters, Alina and her younger sister, Laura. Their only slight concern about our marriage was related to the fact that Alina's cousin had married a Libyan Muslim in the UK. She converted to Islam, dropped out of university, wore a niqab and lived in a housing commission flat in London with her husband. They eventually moved to Libya.

Alina's parents quickly figured such a path was unlikely given my status as a doctor and my enthusiasm for Peter's collection of top shelf Grange.

Taking Alina to Bangladesh after the wedding was a way of showing her my ancestry, but also to tighten the bonds between her and my family. When our flight landed in Dhaka, we were met by a throng of relatives who whisked us away from the army of beggars and touts wanting a tip after holding our luggage without permission. The customs line was manned by elderly men with long beards who took an eternity to mark their stamp, carefully flicking through all the pages of every passport. I'd already prepared for the possibility of paying a bribe to avoid a lengthy, unnecessary search of our luggage. It didn't eventuate and I was disappointed that I couldn't be seen to be savvy with the locals.

My relatives had been practising their English in preparation for Alina's arrival but froze when faced with making actual conversation with a white woman, someone they would usually have called 'maam-sahib', a hangover from British colonisation. A pair of aunts were able to blurt out 'Hello Alina' but were then lost for words and resorted to stroking her blonde hair. My grandmother was among the welcoming party and kept saying 'Thank you', admitting later that she didn't know how to greet someone in English. She complained that I should have taught Alina Bengali.

We were led down a staircase with a VIP signpost. In the underground car park a minibus was waiting. Several sinewy young military officers, most with moustaches, could be seen patrolling the area and our loud group was saluted by one at the bottom of the stairwell. The minibus was from one of Bangladesh's major insurance companies, National Life, its green flower logo prominent on the sliding door. As a mark of respect for my father, the vehicle was loaned by the company to transport us throughout the country.

My father did actuarial work for National Life. They would send him packages regularly and he'd spend hours calculating probability ratios for life insurance premiums. There would often be late night phone calls to the family home in Sydney which made my mother crazy. 'Hello, Madam. Assalama-alaykum. This is National Life,' the enthusiastic young men would shout into the phone at approximately midnight Australian time. My father's links with the industry in Bangladesh had remained strong and many of my relatives were employed within it, their roles arranged by my father via Sydney.

I had organised accommodation at a nearby guesthouse, the Fern Tree Lodge. I'd read in my Lonely Planet that American expats and Western aid workers stayed there. I was terrified that Alina would be overwhelmed by the poverty, pollution and masses of people and would need sanctuary from it all. Bangladesh is the size of Victoria and has a population of 150 million. I once caught a public bus on one of my visits to the old country and had another passenger's nose up against my cheek for the entire trip while several others hung off the side of the vehicle. By comparison, India feels positively under-populated and peaceful.

Just walking outside makes you feel as though you're drowning in a sea of cars, bicycles, scooters and people. Especially people. People walking rapidly down dilapidated pathways, people carrying bricks on their head to construction sites, people yelling at stationary cars to give them room to cross the road, people ogling passers-by without a care in the world. The smell of exhaust fumes and sweat and the sound of car horns and rickshaw bells force out any emerging thoughts.

When our transport dropped us to the Lodge, a man wearing a shiny black suit took our bags.

'Thank you, Sir. Thank you, Madam,' said the suave

porter. He stared at me before moving on to Alina. It would have been rude in Australia, but I expected onlookers to peer at us with curiosity, a Bangladeshi man partnered with an English rose of a wife.

Led by Bulu, my mum's younger sister, several aunts and cousins led us to our room. Bulu told us how disappointed she was to have missed out on the wedding celebrations in Sydney and about the extended family's need to compensate during our visit. 'We will have our fun, whether you like it or not,' she said in Bengali, grinning.

With a flourish she opened the door to reveal our hotel room filled with flowers. Most were bright orange marigolds, but there were also roses. A garland of frilly white flowers was hung across the window behind the bed. The bed itself was adorned with a love heart made with roses, with the letters S and A formed either side of the heart. The S was for Shuvo, my Bengali nickname. It was cheesy, but touching.

Before venturing on to my parents' villages, Alina and I spent several days in the capital city meeting relatives and family friends. Children were often more fluent in English, being better schooled and more familiar with Hollywood. Satellite television, which even families living in the slums had access to, where they would see foreign movies or listen to English commentary while watching cricket, also helped. One young boy we befriended on the street spoke English like an cricket commentator: 'What a wife! Lovely marriage, that one!'

Alina was deeply affected by the poverty, noise and pollution. She often resorted to covering her mouth when she was walking with me in the streets and burst into tears once when it seemed there would be no end to the wave after wave of beggars knocking on the windows of the minibus. There were emaciated young children, amputees, blind men and women and mothers holding crying babies.

I tried to appear like I'd seen it all before, which I had, but I was far from desensitised to seeing children picking rotting food out of garbage dumps or families washing their pots and pans in ponds with sewers draining into them. But I was determined that Alina would not just remember the poverty. I took her to the university precinct on a rickshaw to show her where my mother had studied and we strolled through its large quadrangles and colonial-style buildings, erected during the British occupation. I'd spent several months there myself completing an elective at the medical school, treating lines of patients that overflowed into the corridors of the hospital.

The university was the site of one of the first major massacres by the Pakistani army, a bloodbath that left the city filled with tens of thousands of dead bodies lying on top of each other. There was a statue of a fallen soldier in the main quadrangle. He wasn't dressed in traditional army uniform but in a peasant outfit of lungi, singlet and a piece of cloth tied around his forehead like a headband. The statue represented the freedom fighters who fought the Pakistanis during the independence war of 1971, the year before my parents married.

The first of several wedding functions was held that

night in a Chinese restaurant. Mum, Dad and Tania had arrived to accompany us. I enjoyed seeing my parents in Bangladesh. They were often better dressed and more charismatic than at similar events in Australia. Abba didn't appear awkward and was revered by his friends and relatives. Several of my mother's friends referred to him as 'the hero', a reference to the male lead in Bollywood films. Over the years Abba had mellowed and was more comfortable about the decisions Tania and I were making. Tania was working for Sony in a marketing role and was seeing an Aussie-raised Bangladeshi guy, Rubai.

My mother was a matriarchal oracle, her relatives and friends requesting her advice on matters varying from beauty to the education of their children. She held court in one corner of the restaurant. Her siblings called her 'Bor Apa', which means Big Sister. She was the first born of the nine siblings in her family. Her best friend, Mia, a classmate of hers from the all-girls boarding school, Mirzapur, sat by her side. Amma was beaming, happy to be surrounded by long-lost family and friends.

Every second person waxed lyrical about how they knew me as a child. 'I remember your big eyes when you were a baby and how you couldn't sit still,' Mia told me, squeezing my cheeks as if I were a five-year-old.

Meanwhile, Alina practised her two key Bengali phrases, lines we had rehearsed on the plane. One was 'Kemon ache?', which simply means 'How are you?' The other was 'Apnar sari pachondo kori', or 'I really like your sari'. She delivered these to gushing approval. It became more awkward later in the night when it became clear she'd informed all the women and girls at the party that their saris were wonderful, sometimes twice.

That night was the first of a succession of glitzy receptions held in our honour, parties that overflowed with food, flowers and presentations of jewellery. Alina said she felt like a celebrity. Outside, large groups of onlookers stared at her, even following her if they could. Once a bunch of school children approached her to have a photo taken with us. It became even more pronounced when we arrived at my parents' villages. In the main street of Jessore, the district town closest to my father's village, our driver had to honk and force the minibus through crowds frozen in awe and curiosity. We stopped to have a cup of tea in a shop made of bamboo and the throng followed us, watching intently as we mixed sugar into our cups of tea.

'Aije, eta amar nothun bou. Bari jabo,' I announced, telling them I had brought my new wife to visit my ancestral village. In Bangladesh, the father's village is regarded as the seat of the family.

One particularly enthusiastic spectator weaved his way through the crowd on his moped. He looked to be in his forties, wore a white suit, a backpack and a round, tightly fitted white helmet. He looked like a turtle standing upright. He walked nonchalantly toward Alina, who looked both bemused and perturbed by his approach. I held her hand in a protective gesture.

'Where is it you come from, Madam?' he asked Alina, showing no sign of nerves.

'Australia,' Alina answered, to a quizzical look from our new friend.

'Os-tray-lee-a,' I repeated slowly, in an Indian-style accent.

He responded with nods of understanding. Then he began to retrieve some papers from his briefcase and suggested we might like to take his resumé. 'Please, Madam, could you sponsor me for a migration visa?' he asked.

I attempted to deflect the intrusion politely, suggesting it was not the best time. He left reluctantly but not before finding out that a reception was being held for us at Bijoyrampur the next day.

As we drove up to the reception, hundreds of people lined the dirt path that led to Abba's home. Both Alina and I had dressed in outfits prepared by my female cousins on Dad's side, me in a purple silk robe and Alina in a bright red sari. The ponds on either side of the path and the gathering's military line-up were filled with ducks quacking and jostling for position, while the green padi fields beyond stretched and welded into the horizon. Alina turned to me, red-faced and in obvious shock. Agape, I couldn't pretend that the sight was an everyday occurrence either. It was as if royalty had arrived.

Once again our driver honked and manouevred the minibus through the crowd of people and as soon as we got out we were tackled by relatives and draped with flower garlands. Alina began to nod vigorously and began to let loose with a barrage of sari compliments, even to the men dressed in suits.

Dodging some goats on the way, which were duly waved away by relatives, we were escorted into the living room of the family home and helped onto chairs atop a stage draped with white curtains. The multitude of guests surrounded us. Over the years, and funded by payments from my father, the simple mud huts of his immediate family had been replaced with a red brick building. The toilet, previously a hole in the ground, was now a porcelain latrine. The kitchen had also been transformed into an elegant brick cottage while the courtyard in between was filled with piles of collected wheat and hay waiting for sale at the local market, as well as cow dung which was used for fertiliser.

Tania took on the role of tending to Alina's needs, such as sending people to get her water. A combination of security guard and public relations attaché, she stopped visitors from getting too close or falling victim to their curiosity and touching Alina's white skin or blonde hair.

The function soon became a huge frenzy of eating as group after group was organised in rows and fed from large vats filled with cooked meat and vegetables. Most of the guests were from adjoining villages. Many were beggars. It was normal, and a sign of status, to feed poor strangers at wedding functions. Up on our stage, Alina and I smiled again and again for photographs before succumbing to restlessness and walking among the guests.

That night we retreated to a hotel in Jessore. In the melodrama of our exit, surrounded as we were by teary relatives, the white helmet-wearing man on the moped arrived, approaching us to make further requests. He pushed aside my father's sister, my only aunt present, to offer his papers even as we were fastening our seatbelts in the mini-bus. I wanted to commend him for his persistence and extraordinary lack of etiquette, but was too tired to bother.

At the hotel we were both relieved to change into track-suits and watch *American Idol*. We ordered a meal of soup and noodles which felt like a blissful escape from rice and curry, only to be betrayed later in the night by an obligatory dose of the runs.

The next day, the festivities continued. One of my mother's brothers, Gogo, arrived in a car with marigolds decorating the bonnet, boot and passenger doors. Gogo was tall and cheerful and known as the happy-go-lucky, caring younger brother who spent his time in the service of others. After several days of over-the-top displays, feigning excitement at Gogo's gesture wasn't easy. By then it would have taken elephants or helicopters for me to be genuinely impressed.

Driving to the Indian border to my mother's village, Dihi, involved several hours of dodging head-on collisions with packed buses on one-lane highways to navigating narrow, newly constructed roads as we passed through smaller towns. Since I'd first started visiting Bangladesh as a child, dirt paths had given way to paved roads and bikes and carts pulled by cows had been replaced with buses and cars. Now, it's commonplace to see farmers carrying mobile phones while herding cattle or ploughing padi fields. As we rolled on, semi-naked children chased our vehicle, rolling bike tyres with sticks.

Aware of our growing festivity fatigue, my mother had asked her family to limit visitor numbers. When we finally arrived in Dihi, there was a beautiful archway and flower garlands but we were met only by a set of aunts, my grandparents and a few servants. By Bangladeshi standards, it felt like a ghost town. I walked with Alina to meet the local residents, many I'd known since childhood.

There was Dubloo, named after the English letter 'w', who was my age and known for his keen fashion sense and being a daredevil on the family motorcycle. There was Don, now a chubby young man whose deformed penis was known to everyone. And of course there was Hitler, a distant cousin whose parents admired the leadership style of the German dictator and mass murderer. He was wearing a green tracksuit my parents had given to him as a present over a decade ago.

Alina chatted to some of the servant girls and presented them with simple pieces of jewellery before sitting with my grandfather, 'Nana' in Bengali, who showed her the books of Russian literature he kept locked in a cabinet. Chekhov, Dostoevsky and Tolstoy were his favourites, his passion ignited when his eldest son, my uncle Badu, studied in the Soviet Union. Nana was a man of the intellectual arts and literature of Bengal, traditions that clashed with newer versions brimming with the austerity of Islam.

'They call me names for not praying at the mosque. Idiots,' he said to Alina, holding her hand gently.

That night, the only one we would spend in Dihi, our marriage was celebrated with a performance of singing and dancing under a taupaulin strung between some large mango trees. My female cousin, Mousumi, sang a folk song about the challenges of lasting love and another young girl, barely a teenager, performed a dance to the beat of a ballad from a Bollywood film. She was bedecked in gold from head to toe, like a bride herself. The highlight was a thin boy with a floppy fringe who performed a high-energy dance filled with breakdancing and backflips to the tune of a Backstreet Boys song. His moves, replicated from the film clip step by step, were met with rapturous and wild applause from our small group. The night ended with random, vigorous dancing, including my attempt to teach my grandmother the tango.

As the night came to a close, I could see my mother smiling with joy, watching her new daughter-in-law mix with her relatives. There were cows and goats in the distance, but it was too dark to tell the difference.

12
The House Call

He was lying by the doorway, his arms resting across his motionless body. The police hadn't touched a thing. His eyes were wide open and his mouth gaping. There were stains of brown-coloured vomit and specks of blood on the side of his mouth which extended to a trail of spots on his chest. He was still dressed in the orange dressing-gown I'd seen him in only a few hours before, neatly tied at the waist. The few wisps of grey hair on his otherwise bald head were askew and I could see his teeth, brown and decaying as they were. Earlier, he'd told me proudly that he had no need for dentures. His front two were the most prominent, which was why his two sisters jokingly called him a geriatric Bugs Bunny.

I could see into his mouth where there was more brown liquid inside. Some of it was leaking out of his nostrils, too. He was probably vomiting shit before he died, the contents of his bowel pushed steadily upwards and out through his oesophagus.

I had a nagging feeling that I had killed him.

Three hours earlier I'd been called to Jeremy Barlow's

house on my regular Sunday locum shift for the Eastern Suburbs Medical Service. Run for almost twenty years, it was started by an entrepreneurial general practitioner who spotted a niche market. It did only house calls and did them at a time when other GPs could not. Its territory stretched from the southern tip of La Perouse with its nearby military outpost and Aboriginal community to the northernmost edge of Watsons Bay with its stunning harbour views and real estate that was among the world's most expensive.

I occasionally visited the multi-million-dollar harbour front palaces inhabited by Sydney's super rich, most commonly financiers and property developers. But far more likely to call our bulk-billed service were the armies of pensioners, the mentally ill and the unemployed who filled estate after estate of housing commission accommodation in the area. Some of the estates were situated on prime real estate, which I felt was a measure of Australia's egalitarianism. Why shouldn't someone suffering schizophrenia have water views?

I'd worked in the public hospital system for two years and had grown disillusioned. I'd rotated through the various specialties as a junior doctor in neurology, cardiology, emergency and general surgery. I'd watched my bosses cut people up, take out their organs or unblock their hearts and put them together again, but it still just felt like advanced mechanics to me. There seemed to be no room for creativity or broad thinking. I felt like I was in the military and was resisting being etched into shape. I'd had a taste of psychiatry and really enjoyed its mystery and emphasis on the human experience but I was also writing more and more in a wide range of magazines and newspapers and had even picked up a gig putting together radio stories for SBS. I wondered if I should give what was then a hobby more of a go. When it came time for me to pick my specialty, I chose to run away and reconsider my options.

I began the GP house-call job to fund my writing. I loved the thrill of having a voice and causing a reaction among people about ideas I cared about. I wrote about career angst that reflected my own mindset and received thankful letters from similarly placed readers. I penned observations of my community, about the trend of young people embracing religion as way of ameliorating the feeling that they didn't belong. It created tension and controversy. On occasion my parents were approached and questioned about my writing and whether I was planning to become a vocal critic of Islam. I never felt in danger, but it was clear my words were creating debate.

The house-call work suited me, too. It was a bit like journalism. I liked peeking into people's lives and seeing patients in their home environment instead of the sterility and uniformity of the hospital setting. I carried a silver case of needles, vials of emergency medication like pethidine for pain and Maxolon for vomiting as well as a stethoscope and a blood pressure cuff. I'd fiddle with the street directory, searching for addresses. The job was a bit like doctor meets pizza-delivery boy.

On the afternoon I was called to see Mr Barlow, my shift was abnormally quiet. I'd already visited a couple of my regulars, a middle-aged woman who suffered from schizophrenia who wanted to have a chat about her new boyfriend and ask for some Valium, and a forty-year-old single mother who called me once a month and feigned extreme pain in an attempt to convince me to give her an injection of pethidine. They were becoming more like social visits.

After sitting in my car for what felt like an eternity listening to the rugby league on the radio, I received a text message from the practice manager. Jeremy Barlow was seventy-eight years old and his complaint was a stomach-ache. I was relieved to have something to do. It sounded like a simple case of gastroenteritis. I pulled open my street directory and found the address.

I parked out the front of the simple red brick home in south Maroubra. There were some yellow roses flower-ing around the front yard and a twisted hose lay by the front patio. The windows were covered with white shutters, stained a light brown. I pulled my case out of the car boot and walked to the front door.

An elderly woman in a dressing-gown opened the door and introduced herself as Elsie. She wore glasses attached to a white string around her neck and her short curly hair was dyed a light pink. She walked me though to the lounge room, where another old lady was sitting with a man of about the same vintage on a brown sofa covered with cush-ions. Each cushion had a hand-stitched cover, the careful embroidery depicting a piece of fruit. There were apples, oranges and pears.

'Did you sew these all yourself?' I asked, turning to Elsie.

She giggled, before pointing at her sister, who had freckles and wore a pearl necklace. 'I like to take the credit sometimes, but not when Audrey is sitting right there.'

I like to make some conversation to build rapport before turning on my medical radar. We were taught early at university that the examination began the moment you laid eyes on the patient. Mr Barlow didn't look in great pain. He was sitting calmly but remained very still. He wasn't hunched over hyperventilating, a posture that patients with a painful pancreas generally presented with. He didn't look pale and wasn't grasping his chest, a typical sight when patients had suffered heart attacks. They often thought it was stomach-ache. Nor was he rubbing a painful shoulder, the site where injuries from the gallbladder could sometimes be felt, a phenomenon known as referred pain where the body is tricked into thinking it hurts from somewhere else because it shares nerve connections with another organ.

I'd grown used to working in a hospital, where the ebb and flow of business revolved around expensive technologies that beeped and acronyms like MRI, EEG, CT scans and ABGs filled day-to-day conversations. Despite being taught to use our senses to diagnose patients, the realities of human error and malpractice suits meant that centuries of clinical acumen were often thrown aside in the modern medical workplace. But now I was standing in a patient's living room, holding only a stethoscope and silver briefcase.

'Would you like a cup of tea, Doctor?' Elsie and Audrey

asked, almost in stereo. I liked the reverence that the elderly still had for medicos.

'Thank you, ladies,' I said, but motioned with my hands to wait. 'I'll just sort out the patient first.'

I walked Mr Barlow to his bedroom, where he undressed out of his orange dressing-gown. Under his blue pyjamas and a white singlet was a thin body covered with sunspots.

'My skin isn't suited to the sun like yours, young fella,' he said with a hoarse voice. 'I wish I had your colour.'

I started performing the abdominal examination as I remembered it, looking for moving masses. There was an old scar on his right side from an appendix that had been removed many years ago. His pulse was slightly raised. His heart and lungs appeared fine when I held the stethoscope to his chest, the whoosh of blood travelling across his heart valves sounding like a high speed train. When I asked if he had opened his bowels, he said the last time was a day and a half before. His abdomen felt slightly firm, but he didn't feel any pain and nor could I feel an enlarged liver when I asked him to breathe in while I pressed below his right rib cage. He did mention he was suffering from a great deal of nausea, though.

It seemed clear to me that Mr Barlow simply had a stomach bug. I told him what I was going to do, then pulled a vial of Maxolon from my trusty silver case, which I pulled into a syringe and injected into his shoulder. He winced for a moment before clenching his teeth, careful not to show signs of outward pain.

We went back to the lounge room and I stayed for

another ten minutes, drinking the tea Elsie and Audrey had made and chatting. Mr Barlow sat quietly, interjecting only once to thank me as his nausea began to settle. He quietly sipped his tea, dipping a scotch finger biscuit into it occasionally. The sisters talked about their life with very little prompting. There was an unmet need for company and conversation that I was clearly filling.

Having never married, they'd all lived together for nearly four decades in that three-bedroom brick home. Jeremy enjoyed tending to the front and back garden while Elsie and Audrey managed the pet galah. They spoke of a cousin's daughter who they referred to as a niece, a teenage girl they saw once or twice a year. Elsie described the years she and Audrey had spent in England working in old libraries across the country, binding books and sorting shelves. Audrey reminisced about her visit to Paris one summer in the late 1960s. Jeremy had stayed in Australia working in a tyre factory.

As I prepared to leave, Mr Barlow mentioned that he felt a twinge of pain, but added that he was sure it was nothing. I nodded my head and told him to ring the hospital if it worsened. Then I left, and visited my final two patients on the shift – a dementing elderly woman at an aged-care home who had assaulted a nurse and a Serbian alcoholic man who required regular injections of Vitamin B12.

Now I was staring at Mr Barlow's dead body. The police had called me to let me know. I knew I didn't need to be there, but I'd panicked. I'd been too relaxed. I could have examined him further. I should have sent him to hospital. He looked so well. I thought it was the least I could do.

On my way there I'd frantically called my friend Shahan, the lawyer, who lived in the area. Wary of any legal implications, I asked him to accompany me. Being a close mate, he dropped everything to meet me, but baulked when he saw police milling around the dead body. Such sights weren't common in commercial law. He stood mute and held my arm in support.

The door was wide open and there were shards of a broken violet vase on the floor next to his body. I looked up at the wooden shelf nearby where a selection of old books, a framed photo of a young girl with ribbons in her hair and a silver plated teaspoon with a picture of the Eiffel Tower were arranged. He must have reached out to steady himself when he fell to his death, knocking the vase off its perch, a final grasp just before he lost consciousness.

There were several police surveying the scene. They spoke to their superiors at the local station on their walkie-talkies. I could hear Elsie and Audrey weeping in a nearby bedroom, consoled by a neighbour. A policewoman approached me holding a notepad.

'You right to do a death certificate, doc?' she said, taking off her police hat and ruffling her short hair. 'I don't expect it to go any further.'

In that instant I imagined myself hauled up before the courts, covering my face with a newspaper in front of television cameras. My mother would be quoted saying what a good boy I had always been, my father suggesting that I had been framed. My past professional life would be dissected and old colleagues would speak out of old mistakes, such as the time when I was an intern on a twenty-four hour overtime shift and missed that a raised pulse was indicative of a clot in the lung, which resulted in the death of a seventy-year-old grandmother. I would be seen as a foreign doctor who couldn't speak English very well, sparking yet another backlash against a much-maligned group.

I declined to sign the death certificate. My voice wavering with emotion, I told the officer that I didn't know the cause of death. If his regular GP was happy to do it the next day, he could, but otherwise the coroner would need to be involved. She looked disappointed and walked back to her car on the street. I would be the cause of a mountain of paperwork for her.

My guilt was tempered by shock and sorrow. I walked into the bedroom and apologised to the sisters. A middle-aged woman was hugging Elsie on the bed, while Audrey wept and wiped her face with tissues. They were silent, modest tears. The sight of them triggered tears in me, too. In unison the sisters said it wasn't my fault. He was old, they said. I'd done everything I could and they were both very pleased with my treatment of his condition.

Of course, they knew little about how to treat his condition but their kind words were a source of some relief.

It was the first time I can remember breaking down before a patient or their relatives. The closest I had come was during one of my first night shifts in Emergency. I'd just bought a can of Coke from a vending machine and had started walking back to the ward to see a patient when I heard a piercing scream from one of the curtained cubicles. I peered inside to see a woman on her knees, crying out in grief. A white-coated collegue of mine was trying to grasp her hand. He'd just told her the bad news – her husband of fifteen years had killed himself on his fortieth birthday that night, swallowing a combination of fertiliser and pesticides from their garden.

I had seen many dead bodies before. The ones I'd performed anatomical dissection on as a medical student were gaunt and bony. They seemed like pieces of meat, any sense of a previous pulsating life sucked away by the freezing process and the formalin. The smell was the worst part.

The dead bodies I had seen in hospital were ones I was asked to certify, a common task while I worked as an entry level intern. They couldn't be pronounced dead until a doctor had confirmed that there was no heart beat, no sounds of breath and that the pupils were fixed and dilated. It's an irony of nature that dead eyes look as awake as a nightclubber high on amphetamines or cocaine. The nurses would leave me alone with the bodies to complete the formalities but I usually spent a moment looking at the corpse, wondering who they might have been. I felt like a bouncer at the nightclub of mortality, a keeper of the gates to the afterlife.

In the hours before death, breathing often changes to a different pattern. It becomes shallower, pauses for a few seconds, then increases in rate for a few minutes. It's known as Cheyne-Stokes breathing and is a sign that the levels of oxygen and carbon dioxide are changing permanently, that the centres of the brain that control respiration are irrevocably damaged. As I became more experienced the association of those symptoms became more obvious, and I began to recognise it as soon as I saw it. The nurses saw it all the time. There was usually a moment of silence and bowed heads. It was as if the Grim Reaper had entered the room and was waiting to claim his rightful bounty.

But dead bodies in the hospital didn't feel that out of place. It was where so many people died. For a society that had so little contact with dying, death had become like an illness to be cured, not an inevitability. While it was confronting to see their open eyes and see their faces at the moment of death, there was a sterility about the hospital environment that moderated the impact.

Seeing Mr Barlow's body was one of the biggest shocks of my short medical career. Only hours earlier, I'd had the privilege of their company and of hearing their life stories, stories that spoke of stoicism and life-long partnership. Sitting there, chatting and sipping tea with Jeremy and his two sisters, I'd had precious access to the most intimate aspects of their lives, an inestimable worth that the job sometimes demonstrated in its finer moments.

I never heard anything further from the police or the coroner. I was consoled by colleagues that it was just part of the job and there were umpteen other factors that could have contributed to his death. I received a handwritten thank-you note from Elsie and Audrey, again telling me that they didn't blame me in the slightest and that I'd done a fantastic job.

The House Call

I'm not one to dwell on the past and nor was I one to worry about my patients after leaving work, but Mr Barlow left his mark.

13

First Day in the Asylum

I grabbed a freshly laundered green gown from a large pile in a basket in the change room and pulled it on, tying the string around my waist like a belt. I bent down and fitted rubber coverings over my shoes to ensure they were sterile. Then I took off my glasses and stuck them in my pocket. They were virtually useless anyway. I could see fine without them. I looked into the mirror while I slipped on the final piece of the uniform, the surgical shower cap.

As ridiculous as it looks, there is nothing to compare with the power I feel while wearing a surgical gown. It's like the cape of a superhero, a superhero with the power of life and death in his hands. There are few human activities that better marry physical prowess with mental aptitude.

The problem was that I wasn't a surgeon. I was training to be a psychiatrist. I barely knew a scalpel from a pair of garden shears. In fact, I couldn't cut a tomato without nicking my finger. If a psychiatrist touches a patient's body they're bound to be reported to the Medical Board for what's known in the field as a 'boundary violation'. The psychiatrist is never the hero in medical dramas like *ER*.

Lifting someone's depression with a medication doesn't really compare with bringing someone back from the dead through an operation or a procedure.

Nevertheless, it was my very first day in a psychiatric hospital, otherwise known as the madhouse. The asylum. The cuckoo's nest. I found myself thinking that my working life was surely less complicated sitting in front of a computer screen as compared to a living, breathing human whose mind is deranged. But it was the life I was choosing after two years spent out of medicine pursuing a career in the media. I filed news stories for SBS after winning a cadetship, rotating through their current affairs programs, helping out a senior reporter for a month in the Canberra press gallery and even doing research for a short-lived business program. While I found the television work exciting, most of the other reporters seemed miserable and looked at me as if I were an idiot for giving up on a medical career. Many of the things that at first seemed exciting, like my ideas reaching a large audience and being among the drama of major events as they unfolded, quickly became monotonous. I watched one of my SBS colleagues voice a story about the Israel–Palestine conflict almost every evening. Gaza became as exciting as the grass growing.

Ultimately I'd found it too hard to leave the security, income and prestige of being a doctor. While the movies always implore viewers to chase their dreams single-mindedly, I had started agreeing with my parents that a stable, respected career like medicine could not be scoffed at. Leaving it briefly made me realise I had been taking it for granted, underestimating its worth.

When I look back now, I wonder if the difficulties I had in understanding my father as an adolescent had made me more abrasive when it came to authority and convention, or whether my perpetual sense of not quite belonging anywhere was playing out in my career. Or perhaps it was because flirting with different interests was a characteristic of my ADHD generation, a cohort raised on television and video games.

In any case, it was something of a compromise but I'd begun the path to becoming a psychiatrist. I also planned to maintain my writing and a low-level involvement in the media on the side. My mother understood my passion for writing and encouraged me to carry on with it in parallel with a medical career. My father worried about the lower status of being a 'mind doctor' and its relatively paltry pay as compared to being a surgeon. In Bengali, the job is referred to as a 'pagol doctor', which means a crazy person's doctor, terminology that isn't endearing. While Alina was supportive of me chasing my passions, I think she was pleased about my return to medicine. The prospect of marriage and a family with a prospective partner re-establishing an entirely new career was not attractive, especially as she, too, had left the law to begin a career in the public service.

While I was disillusioned by the other specialties, psychiatry felt complex and more closely related to the social sciences. But it was still like the medical specialties in other ways. It was going to take an eternity to complete the required training, at least another five years. It involved receiving an apprentice's wage while rotating through different aspects of the job, from treating kids and the mentally ill in jails to trying to help the drug addicted, who so often had a mental illness when the drugs were cleared away. And at the end was a backbreaking exam that everybody seemed to fail, often repeatedly. I dreaded the prospect of sitting it, knowing that it had broken many talented people. I worried that it would sorely test my commitment and I'd be found wanting.

After applying to the program, undergoing a short interview and being accepted, I found myself at Rozelle Hospital, in Sydney's inner west. It was one of the oldest mental institutions in Australia, having opened its doors in 1874. Like so many of the Victorian asylums, it was housed on beautiful grounds which exuded a rustic peace. This presumably helped soothe fractured minds. The place was an expansive estate of sandstone buildings, water views and colourful residents. The long grass and decaying structures spoke of past glories long diminished.

After parking my car, I walked to my assigned ward, number 24. Its nondescript name added to the eerie feeling emanating from the place. The plain brick building looked old in its faded paint, like a local ode to communist bloc architecture. I passed a group of patients smoking cigarettes under a pergola. One was an obese man with dreadlocks wearing a black Bob Marley T-shirt. A young woman was asking him to write on the plaster cast on her forearm. Neither of them looked terribly perturbed or distraught. They could have been office workers on a break.

I wondered what trajectory their lives had taken to find themselves on Ward 24.

I pressed the buzzer on the secure door, fiddling with my open collar. I'd been told not to wear a tie – they were considered an occupational hazard, a potential strangling device. I was quickly met by a male nurse, Rob, a white bearded man who spoke with a Scottish accent. He was broad shouldered and wore a pink Bonds collared T-shirt.

'Welcome. Dr Ahmed, yeah?' he said, jangling a large number of oversized keys on a gigantic key ring. 'I hope you last longer than the last registrar. She was gone by midday.'

I had already heard the story. Apparently she'd quit psychiatry training before the first day was over. I was start-ing to understand why. My own doubts were circling and any mention of the work and career in a negative slant triggered them further – crazy people never got better, the career was of low prestige and medical colleagues looked down on you. Maybe I would become weird and crazy myself. I'd been able to suppress my concerns all morning, but they started gaining momentum again, like a broth bubbling up over the lid.

Rob was the nursing unit manager and he immediately shuttled me out to another part of the hospital. 'We're going to have to throw you straight into the deep end, young man,' he said with a broad grin, filling me in. Apparently one of my colleagues had called in sick and they needed someone urgently at the ECT suite.

'Bloody hell,' I said.

Rob was leading me to a sandstone cottage overlooking

the adjacent bay. 'This is where they do it, doc,' he said, before heading back to the ward. 'I'll leave you to it. One of the senior doctors will walk you through it.'

There is no act in psychiatry more controversial or stigmatised than putting an electric current through the body of another human being. I knew that electoconvulsive therapy – otherwise known as shock treatment – sometimes helped people when all else failed, especially those suffering from very serious mental illness, but I hadn't expected to be doing it myself, nor so soon. I'd never seen it done before and hadn't had any prior training.

And so here I was, changing into a surgical gown, as if I was about to scrub in for an operation. From what I could gather, the procedure was pretty similar with a general anaesthetic and the aid of lots of beeping machines.

As I stood beside a knob-laden machine that would graph the seizure pattern taking place in the patient's brain, I felt like a KGB operative. A male nurse, Dave, organised bandages and leads before a sixty-something man with thick glasses walked in. He wore stonewashed jeans and a tight T-shirt that only just covered his belly button. A tattoo snaked out from under one of his short sleeves. I assumed he was the patient until Dave informed me that his name was Dr Bruce Boman, the man who was my boss and who managed the training of doctors in the hospital.

He was a poster boy for why people think psychiatrists are crazy. He was helpful enough, though, and guided me through the use of the machine, setting the various settings to the required strengths. There were was only one patient on the list, an elderly woman who I guessed to be Sri Lankan. She looked tormented as she stared up at the ceiling, mumbling various phrases in what sounded like Tamil. Her lips were writhing in a slow, sinewy manner which was probably the result of medication. I wondered how difficult it must have been for her relatives to agree to the application of this treatment.

I sneaked a look at her file, more out of curiosity than for any medical need. Sure enough, she was of Tamil background and had been living in Australia for several years, but had a traumatic background with relatives lost in the Sri Lankan civil war. This may not have had anything to do with the reason why she'd stopped eating and drinking for two weeks, which was why her daughter brought her to hospital. She might simply have grown old and developed dementia which was then further complicated by depression or another mental illness. I noticed she had already received ECT during a previous admission the year before and had made a full recovery, returning home where she lived with her daughter. This eased my own anxieties about performing the treatment. I felt less like the pusher of archaic, medieval therapies and more like a modern healer.

Dr Boman patted me on the shoulder, sensing my anxiety. 'She'll be a different person within two or three of these. You watch, next time you see her she'll be telling you about her roses.' He went on to explain that patients were usually given between eight to twelve treatments. If it wasn't working by then, it wasn't ever likely to work.

I stuck leads on her chest, behind her ears and on her

forehead. This would ensure an accurate signal and trace of her brain activity. I rubbed alcoholic gel on her forehead and on the middle of her scalp, aiming to improve the contact between the metal paddles I was about to place on her head. It was a technique called unilateral delivery which reduced side effects like the loss of short-term memory. I started to feel a sense of cool efficiency, trained into me by several years of medical training.

'You're right on track, Dr Ahmed. Like a natural,' Dr Boman said, readjusting his wonky glasses as he spoke.

In spite of my initial impression of Dr Boman, I was reassured by his presence and felt soothed by his calm demeanour. There was also a part of me that was a little perturbed that he was already feeling like a colleague. Perhaps I was already going crazy.

A young Asian woman with beads in her long black hair arrived. She introduced herself nervously as the anaesthetist. She was sorry for running late. In an efficient flurry of activity, she slid a cannula into the woman's left hand, a curved plastic tube into her mouth to maintain her airway and then injected a bubbly, milky white fluid into the cannula. It was a drug called Propofol, a medication that suppresses consciousness and the ability to feel pain. It was the same drug that would help kill Michael Jackson a couple of years later.

The anaesthetist gave me a smile and a thumbs-up. I looked at Dr Boman and he nodded his head. I placed the leads on the patient's forehead and scalp and then depressed the red button on the side of each paddle.

Several hundred volts of electricity passed through the woman's skull and into her body. I expected her to jolt uncontrollably but all I could see was the rhythmic sway of her feet and legs, her toes flexing and extending underneath the bed sheet. The machine spewed out a reading on its paper roll in a parabolic pattern. I remembered from my textbooks that a graph looking like the rolling mountains of the Himalayas suggested a more therapeutic fit, whereas more petite mounds like those of, say, Baulkham Hills were likely to be less effective.

The fit lasted almost thirty seconds. It was agonising watching her lips quivering and her leg shaking. I knew the theory of why it was done but, for a moment, I felt its stigma and why it appeared inhumane. The anaesthetist looked on in awe, telling us that it was very different to her usual surgical lists, normally full of thyroid dissections and women giving birth.

Finally the patient's fit stopped, setting off a frenzy of activity in the room. We stripped the leads away, wiped away the gel I had rubbed into her scalp and forehead and pulled the airway tube out before the anaesthetic had a chance to wear off. She was wheeled off and my work was done.

Dr Boman patted me on the back before hurrying out of the room. My other colleagues steadily put away the equipment before filing away to their wards and clinics.

'How does ECT work anyway?' the anaesthetist asked me. 'I'm Rachel, by the way.'

'It's my first day,' I replied. 'I know as much about this as you do, probably less. I've read it's got something to do with sodium channels. They don't really know.'

Rachel nodded and told me that she didn't know how medical colleagues like me wanted to become psychiatrists, a comment I would become used to hearing. What she meant was that I didn't appear completely mad to her, and that surely I could instead pursue a more respectable career like cardiology or colorectal surgery.

I felt I had crossed some kind of hidden line, a trapdoor in a wall leading away from the world of normal jobs and people. I couldn't have been more removed from the armies of people working in offices. I began to feel more comfortable about it, more so than when I'd arrived. I had performed one of the key rites of passage of a psychiatrist, giving ECT, and I think I enjoyed it. Once I'd seen the whole treatment completed in barely a few minutes, it didn't seem so inhumane. It felt pretty slick and modern. If this was as ugly as the job got, I figured I would be fine.

After tidying up the equipment for several minutes, introducing myself to some of the other staff and then changing out of my gown and cap, I walked past the recovery room where the elderly Sri Lankan patient was beginning to wake up. She looked drowsy but noticed me in the doorway.

A wide smile exploded across her brown lips, exposing a set of false teeth. My last remnants of doubt slid away as I locked eyes with her for an instant, her gaze appearing more focused by the second. She gently nodded her head as if to say thank you.

14
My Fifteen Minutes of Fame

Waiting backstage, I almost wet myself. I'd already been to the toilet three times in the last twenty minutes. In one hand I was holding a water bottle and in the other I was gripping a scrunched sheet of A4 paper filled with my jokes. I tried slow, deep breathing to control my shaking. I had heard stand-up comedy being described as a kind of skydiving for the soul. I was terrified that my parachute wouldn't open.

The act before me was a chubby, twenty-something woman in a black T-shirt and black jeans who was telling jokes about being a lesbian in a Catholic girls' school. Her last gag, about how her friends called her running shoes 'Dikes: Just lick it' had just died a terrible death. I suddenly felt guilty for being pleased at the lack of laughter during her act, hoping my routine might look better in comparison. It was amateur comic Schadenfreude.

'Let's hear it for our first gay act for the night,' said the the surfie-looking blond MC as the woman walked off the stage, her head bowed in dejection. 'Our next act is doing his first ever comedy gig. Give Tanny Ahmed a huge round of applause, everybody. C'mon!'

I walked up the small set of stairs to see parted red curtains, a microphone on a small round table and bright, blinding lights that partially obscured a packed, raucous audience sitting on stools. They were all drinking.

My heart thumped away. 'Who hates double demerit points?' I called out to the audience. There were loud shouts of agreement. 'Notice how it used be just Easter and Christmas? Now it's school holidays, long weekends, even bank holidays. I lost my licence going 7 kilometres over the limit on Jeans for Genes Day.'

The crowd's burst of laughter reassured me. I could do this. I started walking around the stage, engaging with different sections of the crowd, made up almost entirely of friends and relatives of the contestants performing that night.

I was too frightened of ridicule and of failing onstage to let many people know I was performing. Only Alina was there to support me, as well as Darren, an old friend of mine. We'd met during our medical training in the Northern Territory.

Darren and I had often talked about doing stand-up comedy but we'd only decided to take the plunge at the last minute when I heard an ad calling for aspiring comedians on the radio. The night before the gig I rushed to his house carrying a pad of paper and pens. We watched old videos of comedians like Arj Barker and Eddie Izzard before drinking and smoking to excess in an effort to spur on our comedic brain cells.

161

Overdoing the stimulants was something of a tradition for Darren, although I had long withdrawn from his antics since retreating into marriage and domestic bliss. He's among the minority of the human race who are genetically programmed to become hyperactive after smoking cannabis. Not so with me. He once fed me a hash cookie so strong that I was still stoned forty-eight hours later. I thought I was going to die. I had to attend a family meal and almost collapsed head first at the dinner table into my chicken biryani. I told my parents that I had been doing night shifts at the hospital.

Darren is tall and gangly. He loves to drink watermelon juice with a straw. We bonded over our shared youth in Sydney's western suburbs. His father was a train driver and Darren used to manage the Coles in Blacktown while studying for his medical degree. 'The staffing of doctors in Australia is a bit like the British Empire,' he used to say. 'Nobody gets fired for screwing up. You just get sent further away.'

That night at Darren's house we agreed that we wouldn't compete in the same heat but promised to attend each other's debut performances. Up on stage, I had five minutes before the flashing of a red light bulb would signal the end of time. As I neared the end of my material I watched it out of the corner of my eye and began my final assault.

'It's pretty hard being a Muslim these days. But I find it especially hard ... Mostly because I love bacon so much.' There were loud laughs.

'Growing up, bacon was my porn. It left the same stains, too.' More loud laughter.

'Bacon was so shameful in my house, once I got busted by my mother after I'd eaten a triple bacon burger. She'd noticed the stains. I had to tell her I was having a wank.'

Raucous laughter washed over me. I caught the eyes of Alina and Darren, chanting and whistling in the audience. As I stood alone, utterly exposed and holding only a microphone, I felt a unique satisfaction that I could connect so strongly with a room full of virtual strangers. Then the red light bulb flashed on, and I stepped off stage.

What became known as the Muslim-bacon-wank joke helped propel me to the semi-finals and then to the state final of the RAW comedy competition for amateur comedians. Suddenly, barely a year or so after the 2005 London bombings, my relatively unique act with its novelty of Muslim jokes garnered a certain degree of interest from the world of agents and media.

I was soon exposed to the mysterious world of entertainment and its backroom players of agents and publicists all vying for the cross-promotion of products and people. I befriended an agent after my performance in the final, a stocky man called Andrew Taylor who was passionate about intelligent comedy.

'I think you've got potential,' he said over coffee.

And so I was to be 'managed', much like an office or a crisis. Within weeks I was fronting up for a variety of auditions, usually with some kind of ethnic theme. If the word Indian was mentioned in the casting note, I'd get a call. The first was for an ad where I was to act as a camp Indian chef espousing the benefits of a particular brand of curry sauce.

I rehearsed the lines with Alina the night before, writing out a suggested script in Bengali, before practising the lines with dance moves and histrionic flair in the lounge room of our inner-city Annandale apartment. Alina, who'd directed university revues, suggested I hold a wooden spoon and wave it around for the audition.

I arrived for the audition the next day at a second floor office overlooking Bondi Beach. There were several other Indian-looking men sitting in the waiting room, all much older than me. One was a retired engineer who bragged about having appeared in a recent ABC advertisement.

'I was the one on the roof who looked up and then suddenly looked down,' he told me soon after we met. I nodded, pretending to recognise him.

The other was a middle-aged moustachioed Sri Lankan man who said he'd always dreamt of being an actor, but lived his life as an auditor. There was even a Bollywood film academic. I had entered an underground world of aspiring Indian actors trapped in technical jobs.

I exploded into my audition, dressed in a golden robe and the turban I had worn for one of our wedding rituals. I danced, jumped, shouted out in Bengali and pouted my lips with abandon. I did it three times in a crescendo of overacting. The bleached blond-haired young man from the casting agency stood before me wide-eyed and nodded his head.

'You'll hear about the outcome tomorrow,' he said, grinning. 'Good luck.'

That evening I received a call from a director. He'd seen

the tape of my audition and wanted to offer me the role of an Indian chef plugging a curry sauce on a make-believe cooking show. I jumped around and hugged Alina. She was pregnant with our first child.

I was in the middle stages of training to be a psychiatrist. Along with writing for newspapers, I viewed the acting as part of my strategy to develop a media career in parallel with being a doctor. By then I was more comfortable about being a psychiatrist and tending to the mentally ill. I was part of a new breed of worker with portfolio careers, not limited to one field. But the world of performance, entertainment and fame had its own gravitational pull. I was beginning to feel like an outer moon dragged into its powerful orbit.

Three days later, I phoned in sick at my Rozelle hospital job, where I been rotating through different wards for two years. I convinced myself that the average patient in what was known as the rehabilitation ward of the hospital was chronically ill, unlikely to ever get out of hospital. Surely they could be managed by the nurses for one day.

'I'll be on the phone for anything urgent,' I told the nurse that morning, while pretending to cough. 'I'm sure I'll be fine tomorrow.'

I had already arrived on set at seven o'clock in the morning at Wahroonga on Sydney's upper North Shore. Massive white trucks were stationed outside a sprawling, three-storey house that backed out onto some dense bush and a river. I was the lone actor and there were almost thirty others. The mansion had been invaded by production staff, cameramen and make-up artists.

After being briefed and made up, I spent the next six hours doing take after take, speaking in Bengali, waving a wooden spoon and stirring a korma sauce in a frying pan. The director occasionally stopped the filming and took me outside on the balcony.

'I need more passion, Tanny. Grrr!' he said, throwing in the grunt as if he were the coach on the sidelines of a football game. 'Give it to me with raw energy.'

I felt like a star, like I was Tom Cruise playing a curry chef. That night I returned home with five complimentary jars of rogan josh sauce. I had made $5000 from one day's work, making my $40-an-hour public hospital job feel decidedly lacklustre.

Two weeks later I had another audition. It was for the domestic market in India and I was to play an overbearing school teacher admonishing a child for a wrong answer. Brett Lee would suddenly appear as an apparition, spruik a vitamin and gee up the child, who would then, to my astonishment, answer all my questions correctly.

For this audition I was confident and contained after my previous success. The following day Andrew, my agent, called first thing in the morning. 'You got it again, mate,' he said, sounding pleased with himself. 'That's two from two.'

My confidence was sky high. I strutted around both at work and at home. Alina commented that I seemed more virile. Perhaps I would corner the global market in male Indian characters overacting and speaking in dodgy accents. The possibilities seemed limitless. I imagined myself in a Bollywood movie, perhaps playing an Australian expat

Indian co-starring with Brett Lee. Hollywood wasn't out of the question, either. I wondered which leading ladies I might like to partner with in a romantic comedy – perhaps Natalie Portman or Anne Hathaway in a tale of cultural misunderstanding.

I'd appeared on television a few times already, usually serious, discussion shows related to current affairs, which few of my friends had seen. They only remembered what I was wearing or if my hair looked messy, not anything I said. When the curry sauce advertisement aired on television, I received text messages day and night from friends and acquaintances. I'd reinvented myself as a performing quasi-Indian chef.

I felt a genuine appeasement of an underlying need to perform, a drive I had long suppressed. I loved being the centre of attention. If a desire for fame was ultimately a desire to be loved, it was because I felt ordinary as just another Indian-looking doctor and of being trapped in the unbending cage of the medical hierarchy.

The shrink in me realised there was a bit of narcissism going on, but I dismissed it as being a product of my age, one where status seemed to depend on either money, fame or both. I felt fame was the path I might use to differentiate myself given money was unlikely while I stayed working in the public hospital system. I figured we were all status seeking creatures and sought it according to the means available. I was no different.

My mother was proud of my performance and reminded me that I'd played the lead role of Pinocchio in a school play. My tail fell off in the crucial scene on opening night. She also thought it meant that I had developed an interest in cooking Indian food, offering culinary tips whenever Alina and I visited. 'Sometimes the taste is better if you mix the cardamom seeds with the cumin,' she advised me in Bengali once, while crushing spices with a mortar and pestle.

My father was bemused and wondered whether it would affect my medical career. 'People will call you the dancing curry doctor,' he said.

His fears were not unfounded. Several of my medical colleagues scratched their heads, questioning my commitment to the profession. Occasionally I appeared on the television screens playing in the ward while I interviewed patients on my rounds. Once I tried to stand in front of a screen to prevent work colleagues from seeing it. One senior nurse warned me to be careful not to make medical mistakes because some of the other doctors would be ready to tear me down.

My big break came a few weeks later. I was invited to audition for a new role as an Indian character in a remake of a big budget American game show. The next evening Alina and I watched a tape of *National Bingo Night*. There was a gigantic plastic bubble with numbered balls circulating inside it. The host threw to a moustachioed Indian man in a black-and-white striped referee's outfit, who would then proceed to say 'No bingo!' in a thick Indian accent if there was no one in the audience who'd reached bingo before the contestant.

I brought home several more tapes and watched them with Alina. She was becoming something of an acting coach. We were horrified that the Indian man repeated 'No bingo!' almost exclusively. The program took ethnic representation back two decades.

The audition was a simple affair held at Sydney's Fox Studios. A host of other film and television productions were also being shot there. Like a mini Hollywood, cardboard cut-outs of Marilyn Monroe lined the walkways and dedications to Steven Spielberg and other famous directors covered the walls. As I walked toward the building where I would do my audition, two men dressed as astronauts passed me, carrying cups of coffee back to their shoots.

A young woman carrying a notepad and prepared script directed me to a small room painted white where a large video camera was set up.

'What's my competition like?' I asked with a grin.

'I think I've met every Indian looking comedian in the city,' she laughed, shaking her head in frustration. 'The producers are going to Melbourne if someone doesn't impress.'

I spent barely fifteen minutes performing several different styles of 'No bingo!', usually with my knees bent and an expansive wave of my right index finger. The woman nodded appreciatively and gave me a thumbs-up before deciding that nothing more was required. She waved me away.

Two days followed without any word. I called Andrew every few hours hoping for news. I struggled to get work done at the hospital, filing increasingly brief notes after interviewing patients. I began to think that what I'd always considered an important job improving and saving lives was mundane, boring and lowly. I looked at some of the patients and wondered if they would ever show any improvement. I longed for the glory of the silver screen and the adoration of millions. It didn't matter that the role was silly and ridiculous.

My phone rang in the afternoon while I was writing up a prescription for anti-psychotic medication for a patient who was convinced the apocalypse was nigh.

It was Andrew. 'Can you talk?' he said.

I immediately walked outside onto the grounds of the hospital. 'Yep. What have you got?'

'Mate, you got the gig. Congratulations,' he said.

I jumped up and down in full view of an obese, middle-aged female patient who was wearing a red dressing gown and a beanie that looked suspiciously like a tea-cosy. 'Woohoo! Brilliant!' I shouted.

'You've got to meet the producers and some Channel Seven bloke tomorrow,' he said.

I started hyperventilating. It was the first time I'd considered it was for one of the major commercial networks. 'Holy shit,' I breathed. In entertainment parlance, it was my first big break.

I attended the meeting the following day with two men called David and a dark-suited man whose phone kept ringing. The two Davids were from the production company and the other seemingly disinterested man was from the network. They formally offered me the role of the

Indian bingo referee. Filming would begin in a week and ten episodes were to be taped over two weeks. One of the Davids thought that a meeting was needed for management to decide whether I should speak in an Indian accent or retain my normal speaking voice. He made it sound serious, as if the United Nations Security Council needed to meet to authorise a war.

The next day I called for a meeting with the medical superintendent of the hospital, a softly spoken man in his fifties. Being a psychiatrist, and sensing both my excitement and anxiety, he was caring and understanding.

'Um ... I'm not sure how to explain this, Dr Snars,' I said, avoiding eye contact. 'Can I have immediate leave to film a television show?'

'We'll try and work something out,' he said in a soothing voice, nodding his head. 'I can see how it might be considered a good opportunity.'

I was relieved that I wouldn't be left unemployed after the gig. I was now considering the hospital job as a fallback to my imminent career in television. But barely an hour had passed before the superintendent's optimism had been quashed by his boss, the head of all mental health services. I received a page from Dr Snar's extension, 357. I called him straight away.

'Tanveer, look, I'm very sorry,' he said. 'We can't grant you the leave. You'll have to resign if you take it.'

Initially my heart sank, but there was nothing else for it. I wrote out a resignation letter. While I had been taught the importance of career security and stability by my parents, I had also learnt that nothing exceptional occurred without taking risks. I was sure that the great shortage of doctors meant I'd get a job elsewhere, but there was a certain embarrassment in being forced to resign, even if it was to play a cartoonish character on prime time television.

But my pursuit of the bright lights and greasepaint didn't come without its demons. I wondered whether I was hurtling along towards potential fame and celebrity with a little bit too much enthusiasm, possibly destroying my professional reputation along the way. I wondered whether I had always craved popularity, whether feeling loved on a mass scale was an unhealthy need. But this kind of reflection was blown out of the water by the prospect of an exciting new adventure.

Rehearsals began only days later. I was given my own dressing room and a car spot at Fox Studios. Inside an enormous warehouse, where the episodes would be shot, there were people rushing in all directions. A fashion adviser organised my outfits and told me to get a new haircut. Apparently I looked better with shorter hair. A bald veteran cameraman called Warren related his stories of working with foreign correspondents in war zones. He said he almost lost his leg in Bosnia when a land mine exploded near him. Filming game shows and local dramas was his way of slowing down.

One of the Davids toured me around the set, a replica of the American design. A large screen featuring a map of the world hovered over a raised platform surrounded by rows of seats for the studio audience, the arena that would be my domain. Big white trucks stood outside the warehouse as if they were taking guard. The editors and producers sat inside the trucks, watching the footage while filming took place. They spoke to me through digital earpieces. The set felt like the NASA launchpad, as if a space shuttle was about to be dispatched.

A short stairwell led to a room where almost fifteen people were furiously preparing scripts, executing contracts and organising everything from the catering to the studio audience. I heard someone pleading on the phone for an urgent delivery of the oversized numbered balls. Most of my time was spent watching ex *Home and Away* star Tim Campbell practise his lines as he stared at the autocue. I was chided by the producers after I started falling asleep.

But when taping began, adrenaline surged through my body. The packed studio audiences were urged to madly cheer and scream. I was drenched with sweat under the bright lights. As long hours were spent doing take after take, the studio audience became annoyed and restless, which sent the production staff rushing around distributing bottles of water.

I felt in my element, often ad-libbing jokes, singling out crowd members and even doing the odd dance. One of the senior producers called me 'the black Vizard' and suggested I was destined for a show of my own. It all went to my head. I was drunk on the modern elixir of fame. I fantasised about leaving medicine altogether and being a television star. After a few days on the set, I became comfortable ordering people around and making demands.

'Eh, lady, I need a tissue to wipe my face,' I told an usher busy with audience members.

'Buddy, get me a sandwich before the next shoot starts,' I said to a cameraman. 'Thanks, champ.'

One of the writers got annoyed when I clicked my fingers, telling him to come up with jokes for me.

Walking toward my dressing room one day, a black Audi sedan with heavily tinted windows pulled up in the studio lot. The passenger door opened to reveal a casually dressed Keith Urban. I peeked inside but quickly pulled away and pretended to saunter on nonchalantly, hiding my excitement at seeing the long, curly red locks of Nicole Kidman. She was organising herself in the back seat while Keith and the driver surveyed the surroundings for possible threats. I felt like I had entered a parallel universe of the uber-famous, the playground that mythic godlike creatures called celebrities inhabited. I would later attend the Derby Day races in Melbourne and sip champagne with Shane Warne and Eddie Maguire in the fabled Emirates tent, having been introduced to them as the 'Bingo guy'.

While I didn't feel an outright catharsis, at the final wrap party I sipped my glass of wine with satisfaction, celebrating an enjoyable two weeks of work. I watched the producers congratulate each other. The taller, more articulate of the Davids approached me.

'Every kid in the playground will be saying "No bingo!" when this things airs, Tanny,' he said, waving his index finger like my character.

Two months later I was back working in another public

hospital psychiatry job. It now felt downright tedious. The doctor as a cultural hero felt like a myth. Where was my own change room? My hair really needed attention. There was no one on the ward lining up for my autograph – only my prescription pad and the medication charts needed my signature.

But when the first ad for the show began to air, showing the host congratulating a winning contestant and me repeating 'No bingo!', I started feeling exposed, my public persona reduced to a mere catchphrase. When the first episode aired, I watched it with Alina, my parents and a handful of friends. I was terrified of becoming a national laughing stock. After the initial promotion, I appeared performing my line, knees bent and waving my right index finger in a wild flourish.

My mother beamed with pride and started clapping. My friends mostly giggled. One of them mimicked my hand waving and accent. As the show went on, I cringed whenever I appeared, imagining much of the viewing audience doing the same. The editing of the show appeared slow and stilted. Almost none of my wittier lines remained and my character was just as one-dimensional as that of the American version. I was discovering one of the harsh realities of commercial television first-hand.

The next day I received a congratulatory phone call from the producers. The show had rated the highest in its timeslot. The publicity department called me all day with requests for interviews. Some of the nursing staff addressed me with 'No bingo!' when I arrived at work. I walked around the hospital distracted. My mother described her workmates performing my line in the lift at the Taxation Office. I was the toast of the debt collection department.

One morning, when I walked out of the front door of the house Alina and I had just bought in Dulwich Hill, a camera crew and female journalist from a rival network approached me. They'd been waiting at the petrol station across the street. The day before, a mysterious caller had tried to confirm with Alina if the address was where I lived, before hanging up abruptly.

I answered a series of questions calmly, was taped peeling a banana and was then filmed driving away as if I was angrily avoiding the questions. The rival network wanted to paint the show as a scam, that Channel Seven was ripping off poor home viewers, promising wins that never materialised. It aired on a prime-time current affairs program a few days later and was deemed so important that it was the lead story after a weekend featuring a federal election and the election of a new prime minister. The promotion aired a clip which showed me saying I was disappointed before linking it with the unfounded accusations. One of the producers from the show told me years later that my confrontation occurred during a heated period between two current affairs programs attempting to bring down the ratings on their rivals' network.

After the first three episodes, the Bingo program's ratings slid dramatically. Despite the fall, teacher friends of mine confirmed that many kids were in fact calling out 'No bingo!' in the schoolyard. My maternal uncle Lattu, who had migrated several years earlier to Australia through the family reunion laws, spoke of a bank branch meeting where the chairman used the line to refuse a new proposal from a staff member. Other friends in the financial markets talked about brokers ending trades with the phrase.

By the sixth episode, the audience numbers were less than half of the first stellar showing. There was no announcement about the program, just that it would break for Christmas. Andrew and I met with a senior Channel Seven executive in January in the hope of some information about the direction of the show, but were told only that the program was up for review.

Two months later there still hadn't been any contact. I asked if I was going to be invited to the Logies, but was met with silence. I'd only spent a few months in the national spotlight, which was longer than the fifteen minutes Andy Warhol had predicted, but it felt just as brief. The show felt like a virus that viewers had caught and were affected by momentarily before their natural immunity fought it off.

My initial cloud of disappointment parted. I threw myself back into my hospital job, feeling pleased and motivated by the tangible, meaningful role. Television couldn't be relied upon for a long-term, substantive career. For the next year I did the occasional comedy act before the responsibilities of family and work rendered fronting up to evening gigs at pubs and clubs unviable, especially since our baby daughter, Katarina, had now become the centre of our lives, waking us at any hour of the night and demanding our constant attention.

I avoided advertised auditions, worried about damage to my professional reputation. Looking back on the entire period it was as if I was afflicted with some rare strain of brain disease, a crazed Bingo-themed dementia. I'd become as delusional as some of my patients.

For a few months longer I clung to my flicker of glory but, finally, after watching a home improvement program air in my previous timeslot, I folded up my black-and-white striped referee's outfit and tucked it away deep in my wardrobe.

15

A Failure to Remember

It was my last chance. I'd already failed twice. I was also on the radar of the regulatory authority for psychiatrists, the College, after speaking out in public. I'd written about what I thought was an unfair examination process in the newspaper. My registrar colleagues still in training were shocked and feared I was committing career suicide.

After failing the second time, I slumped to the floor of our lounge room and lay prone on our Turkish rug in tears. I had discovered the result while scrolling down the list of five-digit numbers, codes for each of the candidates, with either the word 'PASS' or 'FAIL' next to them. It was as if the computer was shouting out my ineptitude.

Alina carried Katarina, who was now two, away because she was becoming upset by my sudden hysteria. I calmed myself after a few minutes, but there was still a gaping hole of disappointment and a cloud of uncertainty about my future. The exam was the final, gruelling obstacle course I had to complete before I could call myself a specialist, allowing me to leave the public psychiatric hospital system with its crappy pay, night shifts and demoralised workplace.

It was my ticket out of medico purgatory.

Failing at the last hurdle would make the decade and a half of training, traversing agonisingly through the medical hierarchy – from medical student to intern, intern to resident, resident to registrar – seem all in vain. It would mean I'd spent the most dynamic, energised years of my life chasing a futile, out-of-reach goal. It would mean a less secure future for my family and leave my confidence shattered. It would be like trying to climb Everest and collapsing from lack of oxygen a hundred metres from the summit.

It had been a year and a half since my foray into the heady world of TV entertainment had ended and I was now engrossed by my medical career. I planned to give the psychiatry exam one more go and if I failed, I didn't know what I'd do next. I'd postponed my other writing and media activities, knowing that I found it difficult maintaining long-term focus. A portfolio career at this crucial time just wouldn't wash.

I had spent the last three months in preparation. Having been through it all before, twice, I went through the necessary motions, meeting with the three others in my study group every weekend to practise old questions, harassing psychiatrists across Sydney to get them to watch me perform interviews with patients and seeking reassurance from exam candidates who had failed repeatedly but who had passed eventually.

I became close to the members of my study group, people who were unlikely to have been friends otherwise. There was Li, George and Katia. Li's western name was

Michael. He had failed twice, too. He was raised in Taiwan and Hong Kong before attending university in Australia. He was proof that simply knowing the theoretical details laid out in the thick textbooks was no guarantee of passing.

We'd sat the exam together once before when it was held in Auckland. The College represented the profession in both Australia and New Zealand. The exam locations were rotated throughout the region, thus failing several times had resulted in a compulsory tour of Aussie and Kiwi capital cities. Perhaps a career in the tourism industry was an option if my lack of success continued.

My first attempt had been in Auckland. Back then I was full of confidence, having been assured by colleagues who had already passed that performance – not knowledge – was the key. Having performed in public in numerous guises on too many occasions to remember, I thought I'd be a shoo-in. The key exam is called 'the long case', which involves interviewing a patient for fifty minutes while two senior psychiatrists observe. Then there is a twenty-minute break to allow the candidate to prepare a presentation of diagnosis and management for the two senior psychiatrists before a half-hour of what feels like life-threatening questions and answers follow.

My patient was an elderly woman who'd just come out of an extended stay in hospital. She had tried to hang herself with a blanket in her room and had also received shock treatment. She'd suffered depression on and off since her twenties, but had deteriorated recently and become less responsive to treatment. She was brought in by my two examiners, both middle-aged women. She wore make-up and her wavy hair was dyed blonde. She carried a designer handbag.

'This interview is not for your treatment, but for the purposes of the exam,' I began. It was a rehearsed spiel that all candidates gave, almost like a policeman reading someone their rights.

'Tell me a little about yourself?' I opted for an open-ended question to start with, hoping for a torrent of consciousness, known as free association.

'I, er ... I don't know what you want to know,' she answered hesitantly. I needed to give her firmer directions, but also noticed an Aussie accent.

'You sound Australian?' I asked.

'I've been here thirty years ... It's too cold and the people aren't as friendly,' she said, her speech stilted.

I thought then that her feelings about New Zealand may be a function of her condition. I spent a few more minutes building rapport. We talked about the weather before wading through the various aspects of her history, including her long experience of depression, other attempts at suicide, medications that had worked for her and how her relationships had fared. I asked her how she'd coped after the births of her children as it's a period when women are the most vulnerable to suffering mental illness.

The patient had difficulty answering questions and I often had to repeat myself. She mentioned a trying period after the birth of her first child, but struggled to give details. I made efforts to be polite and didn't push her too hard, always aware of the reactions of the examiners sitting a few metres away, just on the periphery of my vision. They scribbled notes and occasionally sighed, sending my pulse racing. Had I asked a dumb question? Had they already decided that I was a fail? Did I have body odour?

It wasn't until I was wrapping up the final ten minutes of the interview, the time when I'd been taught to carry out what is known as cognitive testing, that it became clear what was actually going on. I checked her memory by asking her to remember three words, her concentration by asking her to do simple acts of mathematics and her orientation via the date and location of the interview. She had great difficulty in remembering the three words – cat, shoe and piano. She couldn't repeat any of them five minutes later. Her concentration and orientation were fine.

I scrambled to complete a more comprehensive assessment of her brain function while glancing back and forth from the patient to the timer clipped against my folder. On the blank piece of paper I hurriedly thrust at her, I asked her to draw a clock. It would give me a broad indication of whether she could plan, organise and complete a structured task. In the next task, she was able to draw an alternating pattern of straight lines and curved ones, which tested for any damage to her frontal lobes, the parts of the brain that house aspects of our personality, our sense of social inhibition and which regulate our impulses.

I was screwed. She was dementing and it was probably Alzheimer's, given the issue I'd uncovered was largely limited to memory. The realisation meant that much of the history I had taken so carefully earlier in the interview was worth nothing. There was every chance she was filling in the gaps of her memory with fictional tales. I should have moved to the cognitive testing as soon as I had a whiff of her difficulties in remembering her history.

I thought I could still make up the marks in my presentation. I highlighted the prospect of pseudodementia, where depression in the elderly could mimic dementia, and walked out of the interview thinking I had recovered, egged on by the repeated nodding and smiling of the examiners. Despite my slip-ups in the interview I thought I might just scrape over the line, only to find out two weeks later after returning to Sydney that I'd failed miserably, as had my other study partners, including Li.

The second time I sat the exam it was held in Perth. I was much better prepared, having realised my academic limitations. I had read widely, sought out the major professors in order to pick their brains and stayed disciplined. I developed a new self-consciousness when I was in the company of my colleagues, seeing myself simply as a loser who had failed the clinicals, which was what the exam was referred to. Nothing else in my life seemed to matter as much as passing the test, not even my wife and daughter. It was life and death. I often woke in the middle of the night in a cold sweat, the image of a computer screen filled with the world FAIL burned into my skull. I was learning about post-traumatic stress personally.

It affected Alina, too, and I'd sometimes wake to see her sleepwalking, something she would do under stress. She walked around the bedroom muttering things about missed tasks like hanging out the washing or enrolling Katarina into a pre-school. Her eyes were wide open. Eventually she would come back to bed. It was in her genes; her father once put envelopes in his neighbour's letterboxes at 3 am in a similar state.

The night before the exam I took a Valium to help me sleep. I woke the following morning doped out and horribly slowed down. My exam wasn't until the afternoon so I drank several coffees throughout the day to counter the effects of the sleeping tablet. In the first few minutes of the patient interview I was shaking and could barely articulate the most basic questions. But it was more from the nerves, not the Valium or the caffeine.

'What ... er ... What is ... your name?' I stuttered in a petrified stupor. The interview was being conducted in a giant room usually used for group presentations. Settings for the exam were meant to simulate the real environment of assessing a new patient in a suburban office. It felt completely artificial.

My patient was an obese woman in her thirties with red frizzy hair and a nose-ring. She suffered from some rare symptoms – visual hallucinations of flowers hanging off her bedroom walls, and synaesthesia, where two senses are seemingly intertwined. She could literally 'see' the music she played as a child. She was also displaying pseudocyesis, something schizophrenics suffer where they are convinced they are pregnant. She had miscarried twice in her twenties, become mentally ill soon afterwards and there had been no relationships since.

After the interview, I felt my presentation went well and that I'd answered the examiners' questions correctly. Both psychiatrists, a Kiwi woman and a bearded Indian man, seemed to nod and smile, giving me the impression that I was saying the right things. Spurred on by their encouragement I introduced Freudian ideas of transference, about how the interaction between the interviewer and interviewee gave us information on the patient's relationships in the real world.

'She experienced her father, who was a vicar, as a cold disciplinarian which may have made it difficult for her to give me a clear history, given I am also a male authority figure in her eyes,' I said, feeling pleased with myself, and also thinking of my own father.

The examiners nodded vigorously. I felt a surge of relief and anticipated an imminent victory.

But those capital letters, FAIL, appeared again the following Friday afternoon. It was as if the medical authorities were sitting in their de facto English-style guild from the nineteenth century, which was where the colleges that oversaw the exams were derived from, and firing shots from a cannon. I felt defeated and forlorn, a feeling that turned to anger and frustration when I found out that my margin of error was just one mark.

Friends and family were confused by the events. 'I can't believe you're still studying,' responded my friend Ash, who was an engineer.

'It just doesn't seem worth it,' said my sister, Tania, seeing me despondent and defeated.

After spending six years at university and working as an intern that was the equivalent of a lowly clerk, I'd spent several more years in the medical system working odd hours and getting moved around the state from hospital to hospital. While friends in corporate jobs travelled to New York, Tokyo or London, I was sent to the Blue Mountains and Bathurst or Goulburn. A couple of friends from other professions wondered why I wasn't in a waterfront house yet. I'd been a doctor for almost a decade.

Nothing compensated for the job feeling like it had fallen drastically below expectations – even if it did occasionally save lives. Most people couldn't believe I was still doing exams, let alone failing them. Others wondered if I was getting dumber over the years. It was only my work colleagues who seemed to understand. We were like war veterans, exchanging stories of bungled exams like they were missions in Vietnam and lamenting the lack of understanding in the wider community.

Now I was preparing for my last attempt. If I failed I was considering leaving psychiatry altogether, walking away from more than ten years of training. Just like I had perused alternate subcultures and identities in the past I began to scan alternate careers. I applied to become a management consultant at one of the prestigious international firms, McKinsey. I'd often felt that working in medicine left me at the bottom of the pile in a globalised, professional world and I envied the mobile, fast-paced jobs in the upper corporate echelons. From where I sat, investment bankers and management consultants were at the top of the

New World economic pyramid, pulling the levers of money and production behind the scenes. I don't think I was ever seriously going to switch to a corporate life, but readying myself for the job interview was a welcome distraction from the preparations for yet another set of clinical exams.

I spent a couple of weeks reading potential business cases. There was a mountain of material on the internet, especially from America. I enjoyed using mathematical skills I rarely made use of as a doctor, except when I was interpreting research studies. How many cars go across the Harbour Bridge every day? How many light bulbs are there in the city of Sydney? A new gym originally from the UK is planning to set up in Australia – how many branches should they begin with? It was a world away from medicine. On the day of the interview, I suited up and caught the train into the CBD as if I were an accountant or a lawyer. Two different young women, both friendly and razor sharp, interviewed me separately. Each had an American accent and a Harvard MBA.

I had to work out why an ice-cream business was going bust. I had an inkling that it had something to do with its unpopular flavours. The other case revolved around an electricity company that needed to cut costs. I was then given some simple mathematical problems to solve, which I fumbled through.

When I received a call later in the day informing me that I hadn't progressed beyond the first round I wasn't surprised, but it did feel like I was being kicked while I was down. It was time to reunite with my study group.

The other members of my new study group were a young Greek guy called George and Katia, an older Brazilian woman in her forties who had failed eleven times. I admired her tenacity. She told me that since she'd worked as a psychiatry registrar in public hospitals for so long she didn't know what else there was that she could do. I felt sorry for her but also feared becoming like her. She became very anxious during presentations, often freezing up completely.

George was short and bespectacled and several years younger than me. He was training to be an Orthodox priest and was passionate about research. He wanted to treat children with mental illness. I liked being around people who were studious; I could absorb their knowledge and apply my presentation skills on top. It reminded me of the group projects at university – the Asian overseas students would do all the legwork and leave me to present the information.

There was one other person in our group, a middle-aged doctor who had trained in India. He was just like my dad in terms of his career stage. He must have been in his fifties and had teenage children. He had also failed repeatedly and was considering sitting one last time. His name was Viswanath but everyone called him Dr Vish. Like my parents, he had sacrificed much to give his children better opportunities. I encouraged him and gave him tips about exam technique. I told him it was a game and that most people failed because they hadn't accepted the terms or hadn't learnt the rules. They'd convinced themselves that being good at their job and knowing everything would see them through.

Doctors from overseas often resorted to blaming racism for their repeated failures.

I felt a tinge of sorrow when Dr Vish pulled out barely a month from the examination date. He said he just couldn't do it anymore and was ready to accept his lot working as a junior doctor trapped within the public hospital system. I felt desperate. My parents were getting worried about me. Amma called me almost daily in the week leading up to the exam, fearing I might have a meltdown.

'Baba, chinta koro na,' she said, telling me not to worry. 'Life is full of obstacles and, um, I will look to see what Rabindranath said,' she finished, searching for a Tagore quote to help put my troubles in context. 'You are still young and can always do something else.'

The episode challenged our family's migration story, their success in resettling and of their children flourishing on the back of their hard work and sacrifice. One of my patients, who had arrived from Croatia in the sixties and had worked on the Snowy Mountains Scheme, said that he worked hard so that his children could become doctors and lawyers and so that their children could then become struggling artists. I was in danger of short-circuiting that trajectory and becoming a poor artist myself, one generation early, perhaps performing my Bingo referee role in RSL clubs for extra money. I wondered if I was being punished for not believing in Allah.

Alina tried to stay firm and supportive throughout, not revealing any resentment about my repeated failures and how it was like a pause button on our family life. Whenever the study group met at our house she'd take Katarina to the park. She began to talk openly about how we might reorganise ourselves if I failed again and decided to pursue a different career, perhaps having to study again while she worked to pay the bills.

'I could always go back to the law and work full-time,' she said. She was being generous and practical, but I knew she had no enthusiasm for her former career.

I began to worry that failing again could not only threaten my career but my marriage as well. I knew that underneath Alina's show of strength was great fear, something that was apparent at night. She'd started sleepwalking again.

The day of the exam finally arrived. I flew to Melbourne while Alina stayed at home with Katarina. I didn't take any sleeping pills the night before. I slept for a few hours only and my adrenaline was sky high. This time the exam would be held in one of the old teaching hospitals near the city. I loved Melbourne for its atmosphere, alleyways and dark, cosy bars. Surely the town would be kind to me.

Before I knew it, I was once again sitting in a room with two examiners, holding my blue clipboard and its attached timer, trusty devices that had been my companions on a long, painful journey. A thin, tall young woman was escorted into the room. Eating disorder for sure, I thought to myself. But the diagnosis was easy. It was everything else that determined a pass or fail. My interview was a shambles. My timing was disorganised and I didn't complete the tests of her brain function properly.

She had all the recognisable hallmarks of an eating disorder – vomiting after meals, exercising for several hours a day, the absence of a menstrual cycle and the use of laxatives. Tellingly she'd also suffered a heart problem when the balance of electrolytes in her body became disrupted due to her lack of nutrition. She was very anxious.

'I come here to do the day program,' she said, 'but I also try and study at RMIT. I ended up in the intensive care unit the other day because my potassium levels were stuffed.' She spoke rapidly and wrung her hands but her face was blank.

I had trouble interrupting her but also worried about not appearing polite. 'I'm sorry to cut you off, but we need to get through a lot,' I said softly but firmly.

When my time was up, I feared the worst. I readied myself for a last stand during the presentation and talked about the different theories about anorexia, how it might be an unconscious attempt to remain a child and avoid becoming a sexual being, how it had one of the highest mortality rates of any mental illness and my own observational experience about how it became an entire identity for its sufferers, something they wanted to hold on to at all costs, sometimes at the expense of their lives.

I left the exam in an overwhelmed state of mind. I felt my entire life flashing before me: my mother nursing me in Bangladesh, growing up in Sydney's west, attending high school and university, being married to Alina on a hot summer's day and the night of Katarina's birth when she was crying in her crib only moments after being delivered by Caesarean section. Yet again I was learning as much about psychiatry and abnormal states of mind from my own experiences of sitting the exams. I entered into a state of dissociation, like those felt by trauma victims. I walked randomly around Melbourne's CBD, along laneways, up and down the main arteries of the city and in and out of shops, staring at ceilings with my thoughts racing. I had lost all awareness of my surroundings and what I was doing. When I looked at my phone, what had felt like mere moments had actually been two hours.

I came to my senses eventually. I felt resigned to my fate. I returned to my hotel and drank half a bottle of scotch. I still had to sit another part of the exam in two days' time, the more straightforward element called short cases, which involved a string of twenty-minute interviews with actors pretending to be patients. I had always passed that segment, as did most candidates.

When I returned to Sydney, I couldn't talk about the exam. I brushed aside any questions and changed the topic. I was now entering a state of denial, pretending the result didn't matter. Life would go on and I had the talents and abilities to reinvent myself in any field of my choice, or so I tried to convince myself.

On the Friday afternoon a week after the clinical exam the results arrived. They were to be posted on the internet at five o'clock, supposedly so candidates who failed had the weekend to calm down before they called the College of Psychiatrists to abuse the administrators. I felt a wave of calm on the day, like I imagine prisoners do before they are executed.

There was nothing I could do anymore. I was allowed to leave the hospital early and picked up Katarina from daycare before arriving home. Alina was still at work and had texted me a good luck message hours earlier. I put Katarina down on the lounge, gave her a plate of grapes and pressed play on one of her favourite Wiggles DVDs *Hot Poppin' Popcorn*. I kissed her on the forehead before sitting down in front of the computer in the adjoining study.

It was only 4.45 pm, but when I brought up the site the results had already been posted. My pulse quickened. My stomach churned. I scrolled down through the numbers of the other candidates. There seemed to be passes and fails in equal numbers. Then I reached my number, 61422. Next to it was a PASS.

I shook my head. I must have looked across from the wrong number. I looked again – and there it was, next to mine. PASS.

I stood up and yelled. No words, just a roar.

Katarina started crying and called out, 'Daddy!' I rushed to her, held her in my arms and told her that Daddy was just very happy. I called Alina. She was in a state of disbelief, admitting that she thought I had failed when I refused to discuss the exam. I called my parents and then started receiving calls from colleagues who had also passed. The other members in my study group had all passed, which was unheard of. Even Katia had passed after her twelfth attempt.

That night I celebrated with a dinner at a local café with my immediate family – Alina, Katarina, my parents and Tania. I carefully scanned the menu, hoping for a rissole of some description but was thwarted by the modern Australian fare.

I ordered the steak instead, with a bowl of freshly cut chilli ... and a side of bacon.

Acknowledgments

I would like to thank my beautiful and supportive wife, Alina, who has long provided my creative spark, been a rock of love and direction and tolerated my career excesses. If it were not for her, there's a good chance I would have ended up either in jail or working as a rheumatologist – equally distressing.

A big thank-you to my publisher Elspeth Menzies. I had long wanted to write a book but wasn't sure what it should be. Elspeth helped make it happen. Thank you also to Roberta Ivers. The title of editor doesn't do her skills in tidying up the book in a final, skilful flourish justice.

Other important figures in my sputtering writing journey deserve thanks, including close friend and author Antony Loewenstein and my former agent Lyn Tranter.

To my heavenly daughters, Katarina and Saskia, I hope this book may one day help you see the grander story of where you come from and in particular the enormous sacrifices of your grandparents. An obvious thank-you to my parents, who gave up everything they were for their children. A final thank-you to my gorgeous and loving sister, Tania. I hope you feel I've done our story justice.